FUJAIRAH
AN ARABIAN JEWEL

PETER HELLYER

MOTIVATE
PUBLISHING

Published by
Motivate Publishing

Dubai: PO Box 2331, Dubai, UAE
Tel: (+971) 4 282 4060, fax: (+971) 4 282 0428
e-mail: books@motivate.ae   www.booksarabia.com

Office 508, Building No 8, Dubai Media City, Dubai, UAE
Tel: (+971) 4 390 3550, fax: (+971) 4 390 4845

Abu Dhabi: PO Box 43072, Abu Dhabi, UAE
Tel: (+971) 2 627 1666, fax: (+971) 2 627 1566

London: Acre House, 11/15 William Road, London NW1 3ER
e-mail: motivateuk@motivate.ae

Directors:
Obaid Humaid Al Tayer and Ian Fairservice

Written by Peter Hellyer.
This edition edited by Jackie Nel and David Steele, assisted
by Zelda Pinto and Pippa Sanderson, with design by
Johnson Machado, Roger-Michael Raad and Andrea Willmore.

First published 1990
Revised edition 1994
Second edition 2005

© 1990, 1994 and 2005 Motivate Publishing and Peter Hellyer

ISBN 1 86063 139 8

British Library Cataloguing-in-Publication Data. A catalogue record for this
book is available from the British Library.

Printed by Emirates Printing Press, Dubai

His Highness Sheikh Hamad bin Mohammed Al Sharqi

Member of the Supreme Council of the UAE and Ruler of Fujairah

Introduction

The Emirate of Fujairah is one of the seven members of the United Arab Emirates. It is also, we believe, one of the most beautiful and most interesting, with a combination of attractions found nowhere else in the country.

It has no deserts and no oil. What it does have are the best beaches in the country, long sandy stretches washed by the Indian Ocean; the towering and rugged Hajar Mountains, riven by valleys that run down to the sea with palm groves clinging to their sides; and a coastal plain verdant with farms that produce much of the UAE's food.

Fujairah too has a rapidly developing industrial economy, with its own airport, major seaport and oil-bunkering centre, and is now emerging as a major tourist centre.

This book is designed to provide visitors, businessmen and women, and holidaymakers with a simple introduction to Fujairah, its history and heritage, its economy and scenery, and its people and their hopes for the future.

Fujairah offers its visitors a business-friendly environment and a holiday destination without parallel – it is truly an Arabian Jewel.

We bid you welcome.

Hamad bin Mohammed Al Sharqi
Ruler of Fujairah

Contents

Chapter one

Prosperity in unity

In December 1971 the seven former Trucial States came together as the United Arab Emirates. In its first 30 years this small country on the south-eastern flank of the Arabian Peninsula – the 'Horn of Arabia' – compressed development that elsewhere would have taken decades into less than a generation.

Prior to Federation, a century and a half of British presence, beginning in 1820, helped bring a certain stability to the area – at least in relation to neighbouring countries – while the individual sheikhdoms retained their legal sovereignty. But it was only in the 1950s and 1960s that the creation of a modern society began to get under way in earnest. The first modern school in what is now the UAE did not open until 1955 and health services remained rudimentary or, in the remoter mountain and desert areas, non-existent.

When the UAE was established even the most

Above: The flag of the United Arab Emirates was raised for the first time in 1971.
Left: The Emirate of Fujairah, with its coastal strip and mountains, is arguably the most beautiful emirate of the seven that constitute the UAE.

Traditional drummers at a local wedding celebration. The majority of Fujairah residents are Nationals.

basic road network was far from complete. The journey between the two largest centres, Abu Dhabi and Dubai, required a laborious trek across the desert, while the smaller towns on the Gulf of Oman coast, such as Fujairah, were more easily approached by sea than through the tortuous and rocky passes and wadis of the backbone of Arabia – the Hajar Mountains.

In February 1968 the rulers of the seven Trucial States: Abu Dhabi, Dubai, Sharjah, Ajman, Umm al-Qaiwain, Ra's al-Khaimah and Fujairah, were informed that the British planned to withdraw from the region by the end of 1971. They quickly realised that whatever divided them – geography, history and even ancient and not-so-ancient rivalries – was far outweighed by the common language, history, culture and traditions that united them.

The sheikhs of the Trucial States decided they should federate. The country that emerged was small, with an area of just 83,600 square kilometres and a population of 180,000 at the time of the most recent census in 1968. By 2004, the population had risen to 4.23 million people, while modern development has dramatically changed the face of the country.

The previously trackless deserts are now crossed by fine highways and the country is served by six international airports and a number of major seaports, including Fujairah. Schools and clinics are found in the smallest villages, with ultra-modern hospitals in the cities, while housing is no longer the rough *'arish* (palm-frond) or stone dwellings of the past – but well-built and supplied with modern services.

The wisdom of its rulers and the generosity of HH the late Sheikh Zayed bin Sultan Al Nahyan, the country's beloved President from 1971 until his death in 2004 and Ruler of Abu Dhabi from 1966–

The newest addition to the fast-changing Abu Dhabi skyline is the majestic Emirates Palace Hotel.

2004, who placed his own emirate's oil revenues at the service of the nation, has meant that the UAE is today a prosperous and progressive state, whose people, citizens and expatriates alike, enjoy the benefits of modern society.

Garden City of the Gulf

The Emirate of Abu Dhabi is by far the largest of the seven emirates, with an area of some 67,000 square

kilometres and an estimated population of nearly 1.6 million at the end of 2003.

With the third-largest oil reserves in the world, sufficient to permit it to produce at a rate of more than two-million barrels a day for more than 100 years, and with the world's fourth-largest reserves of natural gas, it's also by far the wealthiest of the seven.

The bulk of its territory is arid desert, stretching away in the south-west of the country to the very edges of the Empty Quarter, the Rub al-Khali, regarded as one of the most inhospitable places on earth.

During the second half of the 19th century, under the leadership of Sheikh Zayed bin Khalifa (Sheikh Zayed the Great), who ruled from 1855–1909, Abu Dhabi became one of the major land powers in south-eastern Arabia. In the 1930s, however, the collapse of the pearling industry on which its wealth was based, caused by the world economic depression and the introduction of the Japanese cultured pearl, brought hard times to the sheikhdom.

Dubai's Creek, the 'Gateway to the Gulf', provides a focus for commerce as well as leisure.

However, shortly after the end of the Second World War, the first oil-exploration and seismic teams arrived and the first exploration well was spudded in 1950. It took several years, and several wells, to reach a viable commercial find but, by the end of the 1950s, Abu Dhabi had discovered substantial oil reserves both offshore and onshore. Exports began in 1962, fuelling the changes that have made the emirate and the UAE as a whole one of the most highly developed and prosperous countries in the world.

In the four decades since oil exports began, Abu Dhabi's revenues have been used to fund not only its own growth, but that of the other emirates as well, as the late Sheikh Zayed ensured that Abu Dhabi's good fortune was shared by others.

Abu Dhabi is now a modern city of skyscrapers and wide thoroughfares, of sports stadiums and department stores. But perhaps its most striking feature is the wide expanses of parks and gardens flourishing in the former desert island on which it is built. Unmatched anywhere else in the Arabian Peninsula, this greenery has led to the city being dubbed the 'Garden City of the Gulf.'

Inland, the untamed desert stretches towards the heart of Arabia. Highways may criss-cross it, with well-watered plantations of trees marching in serried ranks on either side of them, but beyond these narrow strips the sands remain as austerely challenging as they've been for thousands of years.

Only where there were supplies of water in the past, such as in the Liwa Oasis and the Al Ain region, was it possible for people to survive. In these areas, especially Al Ain, investment of state revenue made it possible to turn the desert green, with agriculture nibbling away at the edges of the desert in a reversal of the patterns of the past, when it was the sands that were forever on the march. Thanks to the judicious use of desalinated water, as well as to the drilling of wells to subterranean aquifers, the process of 'greening the desert' has extended deep into the sands themselves. More than 240,000 hectares of land have been planted with more than 55-million trees in a programme that's changing the face of the desert.

Many local citizens who now live in the towns and cities grab whatever opportunities they can to head for the freedom of the wide-open spaces, while camping trips and desert drives are equally popular among foreign residents and the growing number of tourists.

Oil and the wise use of its revenues have brought

about great changes and have made possible the building of the modern city and emirate that is Abu Dhabi – but the faint images and echoes of its harsher past live on.

Arabian entrepôt

Second largest of the seven emirates is Dubai, about 3,900 square kilometres in size, with an estimated population of 1,204,000 in 2003.

Lying on the southern coast of the Arabian Gulf, some 160 kilometres north-east of Abu Dhabi, with a small inland mountain enclave at Hatta, Dubai is considered the country's commercial capital and has a history of involvement in maritime trade that stretches back more than 4,000 years.

During recent decades, under the benign yet shrewd guidance of Sheikh Rashid bin Saeed Al Maktoum, the former Ruler and UAE Vice-President and Prime Minister who died in 1990, and then of his son and successor, HH Sheikh Maktoum bin Rashid Al Maktoum, Dubai has grown from a port city specialising in regional trade to one that has won its place among the world's great entrepôts – the 'Gateway to the Gulf.'

Ever ready to adapt to a changing world, the emirate is now at the centre of technological innovation for the region, with dynamic developments such as Dubai Internet City and Dubai Media City attracting investors from around the world.

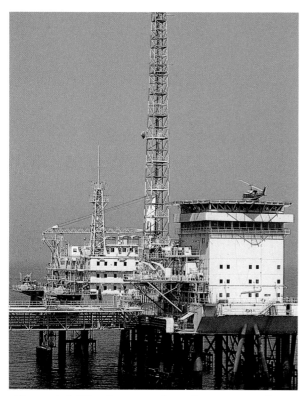

Above: A drilling barge: such craft are a typical sight in Dubai's busy Port Rashid.

Right: Sharjah's wharves are packed with lines of fishing dhows, laden with gargours (fishing traps).

The discovery of oil reserves, first offshore in the 1960s and then onshore at Margham in the 1980s, provided Dubai with revenues to create a diversified industrial and service economy.

At Jebel Ali, the world's largest man-made port, situated 40 kilometres south-west of the city, one of the world's largest aluminium smelters is at the heart of local heavy industry, while the adjacent Jebel Ali Free Zone has seen more than two-billion US dollars invested in Dubai's trading economy.

Dubai's twin ports of Jebel Ali and Port Rashid are shipping centres of international importance, while Dubai International Airport is the busiest in the Middle East and home to the award-winning Emirates airline and the biennial Dubai Air Show, one of the top aviation events in the world.

Along with the development of its industrial infrastructure, Dubai has also encouraged the growth of its commercial sector, in which the business acumen of the city's long-established merchant families has been given free rein. Banks, construction companies, international manufacturing firms and airlines are among those that have chosen to establish their regional headquarters in the city, knowing its facilities are

equal to any demand that may be placed on them.

The attractive Khor Dubai (Dubai Creek), lined with government offices, hotels, banks and businesses – as well as a fine golf course – has been the centre of another aspect of the emirate's development: tourism. In the last decade or so Dubai has successfully established itself as a major tourist destination, attracting millions of visitors a year.

Luxury resort hotels in the city and along Jumeirah Beach, including the world's tallest dedicated all-suite hotel, the Burj Al Arab, constructed on a purpose-built island, act as a holiday base from which visitors

can enjoy a range of top sporting facilities. These facilities are also used for high-profile sporting events ranging from golf to powerboat-racing and from tennis to horse-racing. The Dubai World Cup, run every March, offers the most valuable prize on the world's horse-racing calendar.

The key to Dubai's success, though, is commerce. Its shopping arcades, whether in substantial malls or in traditional souks with spice-laden air, tempt the visitor with a range of bargains from gold jewellery, carpets and designer clothing to the very latest innovations in computer technology. Little wonder, then, that visitors from around the world flock to sample the delights of one of the Middle East's most modern cities.

Culture, agriculture and light industry

North of Dubai on the coast of the Arabian Gulf lies the third-largest member of the UAE, Sharjah, with an area of 2,600 square kilometres and an estimated population of 636,000 in 2003. The bulk of its territory lies to the west of the Hajar Mountains, stretching up the coast to the Emirate of Ajman and the town of Hamriyyah – now the site of an export terminal for

Traditional dhows are still built by hand in Ajman's boatyard, one of the most active in the Gulf.

liquefied natural gas and condensate from its onshore Saja'a, Moveyeid and Kahaif fields – and inland to the oasis town of Dhaid.

Across the peninsula on the East Coast, Sharjah has three small enclaves, at Dibba al-Hosn in the north, Khor Fakkan in the centre and Kalba and Khor Kalba in the south, adjacent to the border with the neighbouring Sultanate of Oman and once a short-lived separate emirate.

The Ruler of Sharjah, HH Dr Sheikh Sultan bin Mohammed Al Qasimi, is the latest in a line of rulers from the Al Qasimi family – a family that's dominated much of the area now comprising the Northern Emirates since the early 18th century.

Once controlling a large naval fleet that contested maritime supremacy as far away as Bombay and Basra, the Al Qasimi family clashed with the British at the beginning of the 19th century before their power was crushed by a British naval and military expedition in 1819 and 1820.

Out of that came a series of treaties with all the coastal sheikhdoms that led to the ending of warfare at sea and a British presence that lasted one and a half centuries, until 1971, although the sheikhdoms retained their sovereignty. At the time, the British dubbed the area the 'Pirate Coast', though Dr Sheikh Sultan, who is also a prominent local historian, has effectively challenged the old colonial stereotypes in

his book *The Myth of Arab Piracy in the Gulf*.

Sharjah was the first town in the coastal sheikhdoms to have a modern school and has since earned a well-deserved reputation as the cultural capital of the country, turning out many of its prominent painters, playwrights and poets. A number of museums, covering topics as diverse as natural history, archaeology, art and aviation, underline the liveliness of its cultural scene, while archaeological sites at Mleiha, Jebel Buhays, Al Madam, Muwailah and Tell Abraq are testimony to a rich history that stretches back thousands of years.

Oil was first discovered offshore in the small Mubarak field in the early 1970s, but the discovery in the 1980s of the onshore gas and condensate fields has made a major contribution to the economy. Sharjah is now the centre of much of the country's light industry, while it's also a major player in the UAE's expanding agricultural industry, with a fertile zone around Dhaid producing crops for both local consumption and export.

Adjacent to Sharjah City is the smallest of the UAE's emirates, Ajman, with an area of a mere 260 square kilometres. The size of its population, an estimated 235,000, owes much to its proximity to Sharjah and Dubai. Like Dubai, Ajman has a mountain enclave at Masfoot, near Hatta, and another at Manama, just north of Dhaid.

Ruled by HH Sheikh Humaid bin Rashid Al

Nuaimi, Ajman is the home of the UAE's shipbuilding industry, with the Khor Ajman yard of Arab Heavy Industries producing its own vessels and repairing others. The banks of its creek are also lined with local wooden dhows under construction in the traditional method and the sea remains an essential part of Ajman's way of life. The fine old fort near the creek, once the ruler's palace and now a first-rate museum, still stands guard over the waterway. A new airport for business aviation will, it's hoped, stimulate further business for the emirate.

Northwards, past Ajman and the Sharjah town of Hamriyyah, is the Emirate of Umm al-Qaiwain, with its main town nestling at the tip of a promontory that juts out into the Gulf.

Ruled by HH Sheikh Rashid bin Ahmed Al Mu'alla, Umm al-Qaiwain had an estimated population in 2003 of 62,000, the smallest of all the emirates. It is also second smallest in size, with an area of only 777 square kilometres.

Although limited agricultural activity can be found around its inland oasis of Falaj al-Mu'alla, Umm al-Qaiwain has pinned its hopes for economic development on its small port and free zone and on the ability

of its fine beaches and sheltered lagoons to stimulate the development of a tourist industry.

One important project, funded by the Federal Ministry of Agriculture and Fisheries, is the Marine and Fish Research Centre, now producing fish for market as well as raising fry for re-stocking local waters.

The emirate's most-important assets are its environment and heritage. Adjacent to the town is the Khor al-Beida, a sheltered creek that is an important site for migrant and breeding birds – and for the tourists who come to watch them – while just inland is the archaeological site of Ad Door.

Excavations have shown that, 2,000 years ago, Ad Door was trading with Rome, Greece and India and playing a major role in local trade routes. The longest ancient inscription ever found in the Emirates was unearthed here as well as a wealth of other artefacts, including a collection of imported glass vessels of international importance.

Near to Ad Door is another important archaeological site, the mound of Tell Abraq, shared with Sharjah, which was occupied from around 2500 BC to 500 BC. With solid stone walls still standing 10 metres high, it is one of the most impressive sites of

With its fine beaches and sheltered lagoons, Umm al-Qaiwain is developing its tourism industry.

Small but superb, the National Museum of Ra's al-Khaimah is housed in a fort that was restored in 2004.

its kind anywhere in south-eastern Arabia.

The northernmost Emirate of Ra's al-Khaimah also has important archaeological sites – those at Shimal and Ghalilah, to the north of the town, and in Wadi Qawr to the south, dating back more than 4,000 years.

Ra's al-Khaimah, like Sharjah, is ruled by the Al Qasimi family. The present Ruler, HH Sheikh Saqr bin Mohammed Al Qasimi, came to power in 1948 and is one of the world's longest-serving rulers.

With an area of 1,700 square kilometres and a population estimated at a little more than 195,000 in 2003, the emirate is divided into two separate parts. The northern part centres on the town of Ra's al-Khaimah and includes a coastal strip and fertile inland plains, while the southern part, in the Hajar Mountains,

includes Wadi Qawr and the villages of Muna'i and Huwailat and borders on the Sultanate of Oman.

The ancient past of the emirate is proven by Bronze Age archaeological finds from sites such as those of Shimal and Wadi 'Asimah, in the heart of the mountains, but Ra's al-Khaimah's period of glory in the history of the southern Gulf began much later, with the great port city of Julfar, which flourished from the early days of Islam until the 17th century.

Visited and described by great travellers such as Ibn Battuta, Julfar traded with China and Vietnam, as well as with merchants from Venice, and fragments of imported oriental porcelain are still visible at the site of Julfar just north of present day Ra's al-Khaimah.

As the city declined, after being bombarded and

sacked by the Portuguese on several occasions, the Al Qasimi dynasty rose to take its place in the early 18th century, ruling not only the whole of what is now the Northern Emirates, but also several towns on the Persian side of the Gulf and the islands in between, such as Abu Musa, Greater and Lesser Tunb and Sirri.

In the 19th century, following the conflict with the British, the old Al Qasimi state divided, with one branch taking control of Ra's al-Khaimah. The emirate's glorious past is well displayed in the National Museum of Ra's al-Khaimah, housed in a restored traditional fortress that was once the ruler's home.

The emirate earns its living from a well-diversified mixed economy, based on light industry and agriculture, with a small contribution from the offshore oil-supply industry and tourism. To the north of Ra's al-Khaimah town the coastal strip is narrow and bordered by the Hajar Mountains, but it widens out south of the town, and has become an important area for live-stock farming and agricultural production.

The Hajar Mountains themselves are among the most barren parts of the UAE and the people who live in them still have to battle the elements to eke out a living like their forefathers did for centuries before them. Encompassing much of that part of the mountains that is in UAE territory, and stretching across them to include most of the fertile strip of land on the UAE's East Coast on the Gulf of Oman, is the Emirate of Fujairah, seventh of the member emirates of the UAE, and the focus of this book.

Fujairah's coastal strip, which is ideal for boating, deep-sea fishing and scuba diving, is being geared for tourism.

Chapter two

Building on good fortune

The Emirate of Fujairah, one of seven emirates making up the Federation of the United Arab Emirates, lies on the south-eastern corner of the Arabian Peninsula, facing the Gulf of Oman. At the end of 2003 it had an estimated population of 118,000 and this number was rising rapidly.

In contrast to the rest of the UAE, the majority of the people are Nationals of the country, although there are also large expatriate communities. Most live in the coastal towns, in particular the capital, Fujairah City, and the northern port town of Dibba al-Fujairah, although there are many small villages in the Hajar Mountains that lie behind the coastal strip.

In the three decades since Federation, Fujairah, like its sister emirates, has seen rapid economic and social development, fuelled both by the access of the smaller members to the oil revenues of Abu Dhabi and Dubai and by the determination of its people, led by the seven rulers, to escape from the poverty and under-development of the past and to build a new and forward-looking society.

Above: One of Fujairah's more unusual landmarks is a fountain featuring a traditional coffee pot.
Left: The village of Bithna in the Hajar Mountains.

19

Although modern, the central business district of Fujairah City is a far cry from a concrete jungle.

The Fujairah coast faces onto the Gulf of Oman, with access to major international shipping routes.

In addition to magnificent examples of Arab architecture, Fujairah boasts distinctive contemporary buildings.

In Fujairah, the process has been guided by HH Sheikh Hamad bin Mohammed Al Sharqi, who succeeded his father, the late Sheikh Mohammed, as Ruler in 1974. Since then, Fujairah has grown from being an isolated backwater, lacking even a proper road connecting it to the other emirates on the western side of the Hajar Mountains until 1976, into a prosperous emirate with a stable, well-diversified and balanced economy that holds the prospect of future prosperity for its people. "The people of Fujairah, of all ages, now live a life that was almost unimaginable 30 years ago," says Sheikh Hamad.

Fujairah lacks the oil resources that permitted Abu Dhabi and Dubai to finance their spectacular growth

and the offshore exploration that still continues has produced disappointing results so far. It has, however, capitalised on its location on the East Coast of the UAE, outside the Arabian Gulf, to play an important role in the downstream oil industry and has emerged as one of the world's top-three oil-bunkering centres, with its own refinery and tank-storage farm.

The geographical situation of Fujairah is one of its major assets. Unlike its six fellow emirates, its coastline lies outside the strategic Strait of Hormuz at the mouth of the Arabian Gulf.

Facing the open waters of the Gulf of Oman and the Indian Ocean, it has access to major international shipping routes, and also to the rest

Fujairah's Etisalat building, with its distinctive sphere, is one of the city's striking glass and chrome buildings.

Fujairah dressed brightly to celebrate the United Arab Emirates' National Day in December.

of the Arabian Peninsula – by road, by air from Fujairah International Airport, and by shipping feeder lines from its modern port. But Fujairah's location is just one aspect of its good fortune.

Another is the sea itself. A few kilometres offshore, the continental shelf drops away into the depths of the Indian Ocean. Here the upwelling of currents provides an ideal environment for an enormous diversity of marine life, including great shoals of valuable fish species. For generations, the fishermen of Fujairah's coast have made a living from this resource and little fishing ports all the way along the coastline bear witness to the fact that the harvesting of the sea remains an important part of Fujairah's economy.

The land, too, has its uses – although much of the 1,300 square kilometres of the emirate is occupied by the massive and rugged Hajar Mountain chain, unsuited to farming except in the valleys and scarcely habitable, especially during the hot days of summer. Yet the mountains, besides having an awesome beauty, also trap more rainfall than falls over the desert areas of the UAE, permitting agriculture to flourish not only in the mountain wadis, or valleys, but also along the coastal plain.

The little town of Masafi, in the heart of the mountains, receives the highest rainfall anywhere in the country. New farming techniques are now permit-ting an expansion of this traditional sector of the economy and it's no accident that the local Chamber of Commerce is formally called the Chamber of Commerce, Industry and Agriculture.

The combination of sea and land, coast and mountains, together with weather that for much of the year is pleasantly temperate, gives Fujairah a further bonus: it is ideally situated and has a perfect climate for tourism. During the past few years, growing numbers of discerning holidaymakers have chosen the emirate as their destination for a unique vacation of sea, sun, sand and scenery, and tourism is now one of the fastest-growing sectors of the local economy. No less than seven hotels were open for business in 2004, with several more in the process of being built.

All of these advantages, however, would mean little were it not for the wisdom of the Fujairah Government in ensuring the emirate's development strategy is one of well-balanced but steady growth, free of unnecessary expenditure on prestige projects, and consequently free of debt, free of cumbersome bureaucratic procedures and yet with enticing incentives for business.

If, as the saying goes, 'small is beautiful', then the Emirate of Fujairah has a beauty for the resident and the visitor, trader and investor, that many will find irresistible: a veritable Jewel of Arabia!

Chapter three

Highways to the sea

THE EAST COAST OF THE UNITED ARAB EMIRATES, and the city of Fujairah that is its focal point, is approached along fine highways that sweep gracefully through some of the most dramatic and beautiful scenery in the country.

The hardy, equipped with 4x4 vehicles, may choose to bounce and jolt along unpaved tracks through the wadis, but most visitors approach the emirate on the all-weather highway that runs east from Dhaid, an oasis town a few kilometres west of the Hajar Mountains.

With farms spreading away on either side across the plain, the traveller soon sees the outlines of the barren mountains looming ahead. As these foothills are reached, a road curves away to the right to Wadi Siji, part of the Emirate of Fujairah on the western side of the mountains, where traditional date-palm groves and, after rainfall, little pools and streams in the wadi bed, provide attractive camping and picnicking spots for residents of the UAE's West Coast cities.

Back on the main road, and just before it begins its climb into the mountains, another track turns off to the right leading to the Siji Greenhouse Company, established by the Fujairah Department of Economy and Industry as part of its plans to diversify the local economy. Fresh-cut flowers and houseplants can be bought here, while part of the production is exported to markets in Europe.

A little further along the main road is a roundabout from where a road branches off to the left (north), signposted to Manama and Ra's al-Khaimah. Eleven kilometres after Manama a road to the right runs to the village of Al Ghail, on the edge of the mountains, from where rough tracks lead through Wadi al-Fara, Wadi Mawrid and Wadi 'Asimah to Tayyibah and Fujairah's

The highway from Masafi to Dibba traverses some of the most dramatic mountain scenery in the UAE.

northern port town of Dibba. A new all-weather road through these mountains to Dibba opened in 2004. The mountains here are still among the least-explored parts of the UAE and the scenery is dramatic. The main Ra's al-Khaimah road carries on north and passes through the fertile agricultural area of Habhab, a little pocket of Fujairah on the western side of the Hajar Mountains, before reaching the Ra's al-Khaimah village of Khatt.

The main road to Fujairah, though, proceeds through the low hills past the village of Thoban, centre for the local pottery industry, and up into the mountains, with its lofty peaks scarred by little channels cut through the rocky landscape by the rainfall and floods of millions of years.

The Hajar Mountains, which run from the Strait of Hormuz in the north down through the Emirates and away to Oman, are the oldest mountain chain in eastern Arabia, with rocks first formed beneath the sea 200-million years ago and then pushed up by the movement of the earth's crust.

Here and there small trees and bushes cling to the edges of the little valleys. At a few points terraces and walls built by mountain dwellers hold back enough of the scant rainfall or tap scarce underground water supplies to permit the occasional palm tree or tiny vegetable garden to be planted, creating startling patches of green amid the landscape of browns and beiges. Occasionally, where a vein of a different rock comes to the surface, there are patches that are almost ruby-red in colour, while the shades also vary throughout the day as the sun rises and sets.

Half hidden in the hillsides are little caves, some of which once held small deposits of rich copper ore, mute evidence of an ancient mining tradition that began as far back as 5,000 years ago and lasted until 300 or 400 years ago, producing metal that was exported throughout the region.

Fujairah's mountains aren't always so barren. When there are good rains, the bare hillsides are swiftly covered with a dusting of green as grasses and plants spring to life, flowering quickly to cast their seeds before drought again sets in. At such times, the mountains become verdant and it's possible to spot plants such as lilies and orchids, hardy survivors from a time when the Emirates enjoyed a much wetter climate than it does today.

The Hajar Mountains, the oldest mountain chain in the UAE and the backbone of Arabia.

Carefully terraced fields amid date groves make the most of the scant natural resources of Fujairah's wadis.

The excellent scenic highway from Masafi to Dibba traverses the majestic Hajar Mountains.

Until the mid-1970s, the route through the mountains was open only to 4x4s. Following the establishment of the UAE in 1971, the Federal Ministry of Public Works and Housing blasted and bulldozed away part of the mountainside, permitting a narrow road that could be used by ordinary cars to be built. That old road, with single span bridges over the gullies and wadis, can still be seen at points alongside the modern highway, built a few years later, which loops and curves up into the heart of the mountains.

Between Thoban and the next town, Masafi, is Fujairah's well-known 'Friday Market', which began business with a few roadside stalls in the late 1980s and has since expanded to include several-dozen shops, selling a variety of goods, including local agricultural produce, household plants and carpets. Open every day of the week, despite its name, it's busiest at weekends and a popular stopping-off point for UAE residents and visitors alike.

A couple of kilometres beyond the Friday Market, the road to Marbad turns off to the left, leading on to Wadi Maidaq and a track back to the western side of the mountains. The main road, though, continues on to Masafi.

The Masafi–Dibba route

At Masafi, the main road divides. One arm turns left to the north, through the mountains, then plunges down through a great wadi towards the plain and the sea at Dibba, the northernmost point on the UAE's East Coast. The other arm sweeps south-east through another valley, Wadi Ham, to the coastal plain and the city of Fujairah itself. In fact, even the first arm eventually leads to the city – forming a wide loop that offers good roads and a variety of mountain and coastal scenery for weekend drivers – but the latter is the more direct route to the centre of the emirate.

Travellers turning left at Masafi, towards Dibba, find the mountains rising high and jagged towards the east, with only the occasional rough track winding away between the boulders. To the west, little roads tempt the visitor into Wadi Tayyibah and the mountains beyond. The geology here is stark and forbidding, but of absorbing interest for geologists, with an intermingling of white limestones and brown ophiolitic rocks, evidence of the gigantic movements of the earth's plates that created these mountains tens of millions of years ago.

A scenic wadi gouged out of a gravel plain along the Masafi–Dibba route.

The route into Wadi Tayyibah, where lush palm groves and irrigation channels line the wadi bed, was once the main road to Dibba but the old tar has all but disappeared and the route is only for the better-equipped, especially after rain. Other tracks lead off to yet more remote spots, while the local inhabitants know of routes that lead deep into the mountains. These are for the intrepid and experienced traveller only and novices are advised to steer well clear of them.

From the Tayyibah turn-off, the road passes above other small wadis with date palms nestling on their edges, and past tracks which lead to the settlements of Wadi Abadilah, Al Halah and Wadi Baseera, before reaching the edge of the mountain chain. Here the great valley that leads to the sea begins to open out, becoming a gravel and rock-strewn plain running down to the Bay of Dibba. On the far side from the road, tracks lead into Wadi Fay and Wadi Dhanhah, where traditional stone-built dwellings are still in use. There's evidence from tombs on neighbouring ridges that people lived here, perhaps in much the same way, thousands of years ago.

Just past a petrol station at the entrance to Dibba, a small tarmac road leads left (westwards) through

Parts of the original tarmac road from Masafi to Dibba can still be found along the Wadi Tayyibah route.

29

modern houses on the edge of the town towards an area of trees and large fenced fields. This is a Ministry of Agriculture and Fisheries research station. Beyond lie the fodder fields of the Fujairah National Dairy Farm. Besides its successful milk-production operations, it's one of the best spots anywhere in the UAE to see migrating birds, attracting bird-watching visitors in winter and spring from Japan, the United States and Europe.

A little further towards the sea, and just across the border in the Sultanate of Oman, a large walled area is covered with gravestones, mute evidence of a great battle more than 1,350 years ago that led to the consolidation of Islam in this corner of Arabia.

Dibba itself is divided administratively into three parts, the largest of which belongs to the Emirate of Fujairah, although there is also an enclave of Sharjah and the Omani town of Bayah. It looks north and east across a bay that was compared by one 19th-century traveller to the Bay of Naples. Up its western side,

disappearing into the distance, are the rocky cliffs of Oman's Musandam Peninsula, falling sheer hundreds of feet into the sea.

Wadi Ham

Most visitors to Fujairah turn right, not left, at Masafi and sweep south-eastwards along Wadi Ham, one of the great valleys that cut through the mountains. The road runs down past little villages such as Bilaydah, with the wadi bed growing deeper and wider. Occasionally it's possible to look down into it from the roadside, although those wishing to examine it properly will need to stop and walk a few metres.

One of the best places to do so is at Bithna. Today, sadly for the traveller but fortunately for its residents, the main road bypasses Bithna and does so at a level that precludes a glimpse of its main attraction. Standing on an outcrop across Wadi Ham is a stern and forbidding fortress that once stood watch over traffic

Niches in a wall in the palace at the Wadi Hail complex, once home to members of Fujairah's ruling family.

The scenic mountain road to the palace at Wadi Hail provides a popular route for weekend explorers.

up and down the wadi. Below the fortress, luxuriant palm groves are irrigated by *aflaj*, little canals built to channel the water along the edge of the wadi, while in the wadi bed itself traces of water can usually be found even in the heat of summer.

After heavy winter rains, the wadi becomes a raging torrent that slowly calms to a slow-moving stream, slips under the gravel here and there, and then comes back to the surface to form little pools that are a haven for wildlife. So it must have been in the distant past, for evidence of human occupation in Bithna dates back more than 4,000 years.

The wadi begins to widen a little below Bithna. The road drops to the valley floor and the wadi's edges recede on either side as it prepares to debouch onto the coastal plain. Here, a great dam has been built to ensure valuable rainfall does not rush destructively across the plain and disappear into the sea.

Just before the dam, a tarmac road leads away to the right, through small gardens, towards the mountains. Once through the village of Gisemri, several gravel tracks branch off, offering a rough ride into Wadi Saham, Maduq and Wadi Farfar, in the heart of the mountains, where little gardens cling to the hillsides

and the edge of the wadis, and where life has hardly changed in centuries.

Travellers who raise their eyes to the mountain tops will find, here and there, remains of little forts and watch-towers, mute evidence of a once-troubled past. More energetic types, who scramble up the slopes to look at them, will be rewarded by stunning views over the valleys and the mountain ridges beyond.

Soon, another tarmac road will penetrate these mountains, running up Wadi Farfar and over the watershed from where it will strike across the desert to the township of Aweer, outside Dubai. While the wilderness along this new route will be affected, the link will cut the journey from Dubai to Fujairah to little more than 80 kilometres, helping to provide an additional stimulus to the local economy, while the higher and more remote parts of the mountains are unlikely to lose their austere charm.

Beyond Wadi Ham Dam, the main road bears to the left and the Indian Ocean can be seen in the distance. Passing under the arch of the Bab al-Fujairah (Gate of Fujairah) petrol station, the outskirts of the city appear, with the central police station to the left. On the right, another tarmac road branches off into the

Bold little fish nibble at your feet as you swim in one of Arabia's rare perennial waterfalls in Wadi Wurrayah.

mountains, leading eventually into Wadi Hail, one of Fujairah's prettiest wadis.

A 4x4 is best for this journey although a sturdy saloon car will suffice. The track leads up over a mountain spur to an old palace that was once the home of members of Fujairah's ruling family. Empty now, but still fairly well-preserved and scheduled for restoration, the stone and mud-brick structure looks down on a fertile and well-irrigated wadi bed, where small fields of tobacco vie for space with date palms and papaya trees.

Nearby can be found dozens of petroglyphs (rock engravings) that date back to pre-Islamic times, depicting stick-like human figures and animals such as horses and leopards. Rare mountain gazelles and Bonelli's eagles can sometimes be seen amid the crags. The palace of Hail and its watch-tower and adjacent traditional village, now in ruins, are among Fujairah's most impressive sights. It's one of those rare areas where visitors can easily transport themselves back in time and imagine what life must have been like in this remote and seemingly idyllic valley.

Back on the main road, beyond the Hail turn-off, it swings round a spur of the mountains and reaches the fertile coastal plain, with the city of Fujairah and the sea beyond.

A magnificent petroglyph with an engraving of a leopard, situated near Wadi Hail.

The fort in the village of Awhala, built on the remains of an older fort, was renovated in 2004.

For travellers bearing away to the right, the road passes the international airport and the little villages of Ghurfa and Rugheilat, now suburbs of the city. Modern villas line the roadsides, but older houses lie beyond, on the edge of extensive palm groves and small gardens.

Beyond Rugheilat, where one of Wadi Ham's several mouths reaches the sea, lies the emirate's southern border. Further away are the small villages of Kalba and Khor Kalba, part of the Emirate of Sharjah. The latter's mangrove-lined creek is the only one of its kind on the UAE's East Coast, a well-known haunt of both birds and bird-watchers who especially come to see the White-collared Kingfisher, while turtles can sometimes be seen swimming in the *khor* (creek) itself.

The UAE's border with Oman at Khatmat Milaha lies beyond, but the superb new highway that turns back into the mountains and to Hatta also leads the traveller to the Fujairah village of Awhala, where an atmospheric fort renovated in 2004 stands on the edge of a great wadi. Under the fort are the remains of a massive fortress dating back to the local Iron Age, nearly 3,000 years ago, while even older stone tombs, as yet unexcavated, lie on the surrounding plain.

A few minutes' drive away is the hot-water spring of Ain al-Ghammour, now scheduled for development as a therapeutic spa, while another track through the mountains eventually leads, by a tortuous route, back onto the Dubai–Oman main road at Hatta. Although much of the track has been upgraded in recent years, 4x4s are still recommended for this route, particularly for those who wish to venture off the main road. Would-be explorers are advised to take someone who knows the way.

Those restricted to a less sturdy form of transport will turn back to Fujairah City, now covering much of the large plain between the mountains and the sea. Large and healthy palm groves show the presence of ample supplies of sub-surface water. The palm grove at Ain al-Madhab, at the foot of the mountains on the left as the highway enters the plain, appears lusher than most – not surprisingly, for the *ain* (spring) bubbles plentifully to the surface, its warm, sulphur-laden water long famed among the local people. It's now the site of a public garden and spa.

Nearby is Husn Madhab, an Iron Age fort on a small hilltop that offers a commanding view over the plain for those with the energy to climb the steep slopes to reach it. Another large expanse of palm groves is presided over by the magnificent Fujairah Castle,

Buyers and sellers haggle at the Friday Market. The variety of fresh fruit and vegetables on offer is amazing.

a great stone and mud-brick edifice that stands on a knoll overlooking the plain. Dating back to the 17th century, it has recently been restored. At its foot are the old, roofless houses of the original settlement, many of which are now being restored as a heritage village, while a walk between the neighbouring palm gardens provides access to a shady oasis.

Most first-time visitors to Fujairah pass straight through the city's only street of high-rise buildings, including the Etisalat Tower, Fujairah Tower,

Fujairah Trade Centre and the Siji Hotel, to the new corniche and the sea, perhaps checking in quickly at the Hilton Hotel, the smallest Hilton in the world, before rushing across the shell-strewn beach to dive into the tumbling breakers of the Indian Ocean.

North up the coast

From Fujairah a coastal road runs northwards to Dibba, the northernmost part of the emirate. Passing the extensive compound of the Beach Motel, on the right, it reaches the modern Port of Fujairah and the Fujairah Free Zone. The former is one of the world's top container ports, while nearly a billion UAE dirhams have been invested in the free zone by companies from around the world. Beyond are oil-storage tanks and a refinery, supplying the dozens of ships that lie anchored offshore – the Fujairah anchorage being one of the world's top-three bunkering ports, along with those at Rotterdam and Singapore.

To the west, against the mountains, a splash of

green woodland marks the Qurrayah Pools, a popular spot for visiting bird-watchers, with the little village of Qurrayah beyond. Here traditional fishing boats can be seen pulled up on the beach, while the local fishermen have discovered that lay-bys designed for motorists are ideal places in which to lay out their nets. Occasionally, too, you'll see the day's haul of sardines, their silvery sides drying, almost frying, in the sun.

From Qurrayah, a tarmac road runs inland past the modern houses of the new town to Wadi Safad,

by-passing a new water-retention sluice and winding through the mountains, a small village and past palm groves and a hilltop fort. Just beyond the last settlement, a dam has been built to store the occasional winter rainfall. For the most part, though, this wadi remains quiet and undisturbed, an ideal stopping-off point for a ramble over the mountains for those who have the energy, and the footwear, to try it.

North of Qurrayah along the coastal road are the villages of Mirbah and Qidfa. Site of a major new

power-generation and desalination complex built by the Union Water and Electricity Company, Qidfa is now providing electricity to much of the Northern Emirates as well as millions of gallons of water a day to Abu Dhabi's inland oasis city of Al Ain.

The plant, though, is well concealed by traditional palm groves and gardens, still cultivated as they have been for centuries. The main road itself is lined with impressive modern villas and a growing number of small shops, evidence of the way in which prosperity is now spreading along the whole of the East Coast.

Hidden in woodland to the left-hand (western) side of the road is the smaller village of Qirath, sleepy and rarely troubled by visitors, while from Qidfa itself, another tarmac road turns left into the Omani enclave of Wadi Madha. Just beyond, a spur of the Hajar Mountains swoops down to the coast, with the road itself climbing over a man-made col and down into the town of Khor Fakkan, part of Sharjah, ringed by the mountains. Beyond Khor Fakkan, the road rises over a mountain spur again, then down onto the coastal plain past the village of Luluyyah, also part of Sharjah.

A little further on, signposts point the way along a tarmac road to Fujairah's Wadi Wurrayah, where a spring emerging from the rock supplies a stream and the UAE's only perennial waterfall. The pool below it is a popular spot, best visited during the week, rather than at weekends when it can get crowded.

The next settlement of any importance along the coast is the village of Bidiya, home of Fujairah's – and the UAE's – oldest place of worship. Still in use and recently renovated, the so-called Ottoman Mosque dates back to the mid-17th century and has a unique design, with four small domes held up by a massive central pillar.

Visitors from all over the Emirates come to visit this mosque which, with the two small watch-towers on the hill behind, is one of the most photogenic – and photographed – spots in the country. Its name, confusingly, has nothing to do with the Ottoman Turks, but is a corruption of the name of the man reputed to have built it, one Othman.

Although many will rush through Bidiya on their way north, the wiser traveller will stop and have a look round. By the roadside is a simple open-air fruit-and-vegetable market, filled with the produce of local farmers and offering another attractive photograph for any visitor with a camera, while a track down through the palm groves to the right (east) of the road leads to the shore and a picturesque little fishing port.

Not far from the Ottoman Mosque, behind the houses, are the remains of a small fort built by the Portuguese in the 16th century, while in the midst of a nearby Muslim graveyard is a long, stone collective tomb that dates back more than 3,000 years. Although evidence of Fujairah's ancient inhabitants is found throughout the mountains and along the coastal plain, the group of archaeological sites at Bidiya provides a better idea than most of the emirate's antiquity.

The recently restored 'Ottoman Mosque' at Bidiya, the oldest mosque still in use in the Emirates.

The coastal road winds on, past the village of Sharm, with its fishing boats pulled up on the sand, and with a 3,500-year-old tomb hidden among the palm groves, and on towards the village of Aqqah. Here a new main road curves inland through the mountains, while Aqqah itself is being developed as a tourist resort. Its beach is beloved of swimmers, campers and shell collectors alike. Just offshore, the waters around the pyramid-shaped Snoopy Rock provide some of the best snorkelling to be found anywhere in the Emirates.

Aqqah's Sandy Beach Motel has long been popular among holidaymakers, while Le Meridien Al Aqqah Beach Resort, a major new holiday complex owned by Emirates airline, attracts thousands more visitors to this delightful spot.

Beyond Aqqah, the road cuts behind the village of Dhadnah and past Rul Dhadnah, with the mountains away to the left and little farms dotting the coastal plain on either side. Inland, a tarmac road leads to a modern dam in Wadi Zikt, where the jagged crests of the mountains are reflected in the still waters of the artificial lake.

Most travellers, however, will choose to proceed northwards to Ra's Dhadnah. Here, the road bears westwards to enter the Bay of Dibba, with the mountains of the Musandam Peninsula beyond. In recent years Dibba, Fujairah's second-largest town, has grown rapidly, with a fine holiday resort on the beach, although the traditional pursuits of fishing and farming still provide a livelihood for most of its inhabitants.

The circular journey along the coast from Fujairah to Dibba, then up to Masafi and back down Wadi Ham to Fujairah, offers spectacular scenery, yet is sufficiently short that a leisurely drive of a couple of hours or so will complete it comfortably.

With plans for a widening of the Dibba–Masafi Road now being drawn up, the journey should become even easier – and safer too – for this accident-prone stretch of highway.

Visitors will be well rewarded if they yield to the temptation to stop at a beach here, a palm grove there, or venture up one of the lesser tarmac roads leading into the hidden wadis of the mountains. For, unlike the highways in the rest of the UAE, the scenery along the Masafi–Fujairah–Dibba loop is such that no one with an eye for his or her surroundings can fail to be impressed, be it on the first or even the 50th journey.

The fort at Bithna commands the strategic Wadi Ham route through the Hajar Mountains.

The old road from Masafi to Dibba, which passes through Wadi Tayyibah, is now an interesting 4x4 route.

Chapter four

The spirit of independence

The dominant demographic group in the Emirate of Fujairah – and indeed the whole of the United Arab Emirates' East Coast and its rugged neighbouring mountains – is the Sharqiyyin tribe, whose paramount chief is the Ruler, HH Sheikh Hamad bin Mohammed Al Sharqi.

Tracing its origins back to Yemen, the Sharqiyyin are also a member of the Hinawi tribal confederation in the great Hinawi-Ghafiri division that divided

Above: Sheikh Mohammed bin Hamad Al Sharqi, Fujairah's first independent ruler.
Left: Awhala Fort helped the Sharqiyyin tribe control the Wadi Qawr route through the mountains.

41

south-eastern Arabia in the 17th and 18th centuries. In terms of ancient genealogy it's also one of the Azdite group of tribes and descended, according to tribal tradition, from Malik bin Fahm. The tribe dates back its arrival in the area now comprising Fujairah to some 2,000 years ago, following the collapse of the great Mareb Dam in Yemen.

Their cousins, the Shihuh, another important UAE tribe, said to be descended from Shahha bin Malik, live north of Dibba in the mountain highlands of the Musandam Peninsula. In their remote mountain valleys, the Sharqiyyin were relatively insulated from the impact of the outside world. Although Persians, Portuguese, Dutch and other foreign powers arrived in the area, they generally confined their presence to the coast.

Evidence of a small Portuguese fort at Bidiya and a larger one at Dibba – an important trading port some 2,000 years ago and once the capital of Oman – underlines the fact that the mountains themselves, and their people, remained more or less autonomous.

The strength of the Sharqiyyin lay in their control of several strategic wadis through the mountains. One, Wadi Ham, runs inland from Fujairah past Bithna to Masafi and links up with another route through the western side of the Hajar Mountains to the plains of the Arabian Gulf coast. From time to time, such as during a regional war in the 18th century, Wadi Ham saw important battles, with the Sharqiyyin fighting to ensure they retained their freedom and control of the route through the mountains.

The Sharqiyyin also held another village, at Awhala in the south, which controlled another route through the mountains, via Wadi Qawr and Wadi Mai to the fertile plains of the Batinah Coast of Oman. The Iron Age fortress at Awhala testifies that the strategic importance of this route dates back thousands of years.

Dominating two key routes through the mountains, the Sharqiyyin had political importance beyond their numbers – although they were one of the largest tribes in what now comprises the UAE. At the beginning of the 20th century, for example, they were second only in size to the major Bani Yas tribal confederation that dominated the sheikhdoms of Abu Dhabi and Dubai.

Unity in struggle

Although they were once divided into fractious groups, as much as anything else by the forbidding nature of the terrain, the Sharqiyyin found unity in

The door of a watch-tower guarding the old palace in Wadi Hail.

The remains of the old village of Zikt, now replaced by a village nearer to the coast.

struggling to preserve their independence.

For more than 200 years, their leaders have come from the powerful Hafaitat subsection of the tribe. With the exception of a short five-year reign by the current ruler's uncle, Sheikh Saif bin Hamad Al Sharqi, in the 1930s, the Hafaitat leaders have enjoyed long reigns, with only seven being recorded during the last 250 years, providing stable leadership that has done much to lay the foundations for the emergence of the emirate of today.

Mattar, the first headman of the Hafaitat to appear in historical records, lived in the middle-to-late 18th century. By 1798 or so, when the Omani Imam Sultan El Imam Ahmed attacked Dibba by sea, killing many of the Sharqiyyin, Mattar's son, Mohammed, had succeeded his father.

In 1803 Mohammed, referred to in Omani history as 'Muhammad-bin-Matar, esh-Sharky, the Sahib of el-Fujairah', is reported to have performed the Haj pilgrimage to Mecca. A few years later, Mattar is believed to have been involved in fighting between the Omani Imam and the Al-Qasimi Sheikh, Sultan bin Saqr, at Khor Fakkan.

Mattar was succeeded as 'Sahib of el-Fujairah' by his son, Abdullah, the real founder of today's emirate,

who consolidated the unity among the Sharqiyyin that continues to this day. Historical records of the period are few and far between, but Sheikh Abdullah appears to have come to power some time in the first half of the 19th century, ruling for several decades until he died in 1888.

He was succeeded by his son Sheikh Hamad, the grandfather of today's ruler, who struggled resolutely for the formal recognition of Fujairah's independence for more than 40 years, until his death in 1932. The sheikhdom, at that time unrecognised by the British authorities who'd been present in the region since the 1820s, grew steadily to encompass the bulk of the mountain region and also most of the East Coast.

One confrontation in the 1920s involved a clash with the British that left a permanent mark on Fujairah. A minor incident had developed into a test of wills between Sheikh Hamad and the British Political Resident in the Gulf, Lt Col Prideaux. When Sheikh Hamad declined to comply with the terms of an ultimatum from the Resident, British ships were ordered to steam to Fujairah. On April 19, 1925, armed parties were sent briefly ashore, while the next day the ships were ordered to bombard Fujairah Castle, severely damaging the three towers facing the sea.

The ship's log of one of the vessels involved, HMS *Cyclamen*, records, tersely: "13.30. Commenced bombarding Sheikh's fort, Fujairah. Expended 4 rounds common shell and 132 rounds lyddite. 15.20. Ceased firing." One occupant was badly wounded while Sheikh Hamad's daughter-in-law, who was ill, died while being evacuated from the castle.

The incident was the last time British gunboats opened fire in the Gulf of Oman. Until the recent restoration of the castle, when the towers on the seaward side were reconstructed with concrete, the evidence of the shelling could still be seen.

The British then sailed away, and Sheikh Hamad's rule over the virtually independent sheikhdom re-mained unchallenged, even if it was to take the British nearly 30 years more before they were to formally acknowledge Fujairah's independence.

During the course of the following few years, the sheikhdom continued to grow in size, with the Sharqiyyin extending their influence to the western side of the Hajar Mountains, in the Wadi Siji area, and further north, inland from Ra's al-Khaimah, at Habhab, and becoming the strongest force by far in the mountains.

The reality of Fujairah's independence could not be ignored forever and, in 1952, finally conceding the obvious, the British recognised it as the seventh of the Trucial States. Sheikh Hamad bin Abdullah Al Shar-

in February 1968, the British announced they would leave the Gulf by the end of 1971, the rulers of the two largest states, Sheikh Zayed bin Sultan Al Nahyan of Abu Dhabi and Sheikh Rashid bin Saeed Al Maktoum of Dubai, decided to form a Federation and invited the other rulers to join. Sheikh Mohammed avidly supported the concept.

On the establishment of the UAE in 1971, he became a member of the new Supreme Council of Rulers, while his son and Crown Prince, Sheikh Hamad bin Mohammed Al Sharqi, took up the post of federal Minister of Agriculture and Fisheries.

Sheikh Mohammed died in 1974, his rule having spanned a period of nearly three decades during which Fujairah finally took its rightful place as a distinct political entity. He was succeeded as ruler by Sheikh Hamad who, following in the tradition of his forefathers, has guided the development of his emirate for the last 30 years.

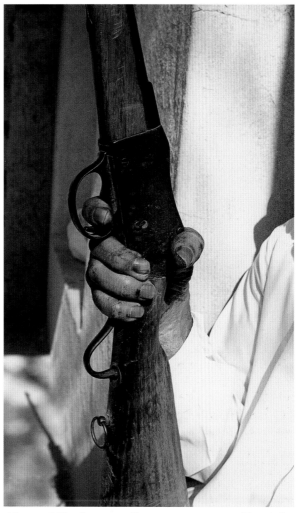

qi, the founder of that independence, did not live to see the fruit of his efforts. He died at a ripe old age in 1932, and was briefly succeeded by a son, Sheikh Saif bin Hamad Al Sharqi, who died in 1937, and was followed by his younger brother, Sheikh Mohammed bin Hamad Al Sharqi.

Sheikh Mohammed led Fujairah through the 1940s, 1950s and 1960s, into the beginnings of modern development and, in association with the rulers of the other six Trucial States, into the Federation of the United Arab Emirates in 1971.

The 1950s had seen a gradual growth of closer links among the rulers, initially within the framework of the Trucial States Council, on which they all sat. When,

Above: Old rifles are still seen on occasion in Fujairah.
Top left: The massive stone and mud-brick walls of Fujairah Castle reflect the golden dawn light.

45

Chapter five

A distant past

Despite its relatively small size, the Emirate of Fujairah has a wealth of archaeological and historical sites that prove people have successfully lived along the coast and in the Hajar Mountains for thousands of years. Archaeological surveys carried out in the emirate have revealed hundreds of separate sites, including more than 500 ancient tombs of different types, as well as castles, forts, abandoned villages and extensive ancient hillside terraces, while there's also evidence of industrial-scale copper mining having taken place in the mountains for nearly 5,000 years.

The great forts of Bithna and Fujairah, as well as smaller forts such as those at Wadi Safad, Qurrayah, Wadi Saham, Awhala and Maidaq, and the watch-towers that stand guard over almost every village, retained their function as defensive bastions until recent times. Although they date back only a few hundred years, many of them are built on much older foundations.

For the archaeologist, however, mere centuries are but fleeting moments, and it is necessary to travel back thousands, rather than hundreds, of years to find

Above: The entrance to an Iron Age tomb, situated in a large graveyard in Bidiya.
Left: Situated elsewhere in Bidiya are these walls of an ancient tower, more than 4,000-years old.

47

The strategically placed fortress at Bithna, which once stood watch over traffic up and down Wadi Ham.

evidence of Fujairah's early residents.

Elsewhere in south-eastern Arabia, as far as we can tell, man appears to have first come onto the scene perhaps 8,000 or 9,000 years ago – nomadic hunter-gatherers whose presence can be detected through the flint implements that have been found in the desert or on the edge of the mountains. At the time, it seems the climate was gentler, with more rainfall and, consequently, more vegetation, permitting wild animals to flourish.

It was not until around 5500 BC, however, that the first signs of permanent human settlement can be traced in the Emirates, with sites linked to Mesopotamia's 'Ubaid culture having been found along the Arabian Gulf coast at Ra's al-Khaimah and Sharjah – and on offshore islands such as Dalma, Ghagha' and Marawah.

On the East Coast, ancient middens (dumps of shells harvested by coastal dwellers) with fine stone tools have been found at Khor Kalba, just above an old shoreline that lies a couple of metres or so above the present sea level. Evidence of the same shoreline has been identified on the edge of the mountains between Fujairah and Qurrayah, and near Aqqah, where flint tools left by Fujairah's first inhabitants

more than 7,000 years ago have been discovered.

Some 5,000 years ago a new culture had emerged in the Emirates as a result of the inhabitants discovering how to mine the copper ore found in the Hajar Mountains. Exporting the copper by sea to Mesopotamia, the people of the Emirates learned, in turn, how to build large stone collective graves. The best known are on Jebel Hafit, near Al Ain, and have given their name to the 'Jebel Hafit' culture.

Other graves that may be of similar vintage occur throughout Fujairah. Some, such as several fenced off close to the modern road running inland from Qurrayah into Wadi Safad, are on the coastal plain. Others are situated further in the mountains: on a hillside in Wadi Fay near Dibba, on the plain at Awhala, in the south of Fujairah and elsewhere. None, though, have been excavated to yield their secrets.

Evidence from the Jebel Hafit graves, and from others of the same date further south in Oman, have shown that a network of trade routes must have existed that ran along the edge of the mountains, and through the main wadis to the Gulf of Oman and the Indian Ocean, linking up with other routes across the desert to points on the Arabian Gulf coast.

The wadi routes past Bithna and Awhala are

Petroglyphs in the mountains are evidence of early art and of the people and creatures that inhabited them.

Petroglyphs are also a window to the past. This one seems to depict men riding both horses and camels.

Dating back to around 1000 BC, a tomb at Qidfa yielded a vast hoard of artefacts, including this jar.

likely to have been in use during this period. By the middle of the third-millennium BC (around 2500 BC), a port town had been established at Umm al-Nar, near the present-day city of Abu Dhabi, which excavations have shown was trading not only with Mesopotamia but also as far as the Indus Valley.

Copper from the mountains appears to have been its main export, although diorite, a hard stone used for making statues, was also exported.

Links with the Umm al-Nar culture

The Umm al-Nar culture, as it is known, is characterised by massive circular stone tombs, capable of holding 200 or more individual burials, and by large walled settlements, such as that at Hili, near Al Ain. Traces of a settlement with a large circular stone tower from this period were found in the Fujairah village of Bidiya in 1987.

In a patch of open ground behind the row of shops that line the main coast road through the village, excavations undertaken by archaeologists from Al Ain's Department of Antiquities and Tourism uncovered the remains of a great stone-built round tower that was almost identical in its plan and manner of construction to a tower at Hili.

The tower was probably the centre of a settlement, indicating that the present village of Bidiya lies on a site that has been occupied for more than 4,000 years.

In a nearby Muslim graveyard, a scatter of pottery from the third-millennium BC has been found and a raised mound, as yet unexcavated, may well conceal a circular tomb of the Umm al-Nar type.

Copper mining in the Emirates pre-dates the Islamic era but had a revival about 900 years ago.

During the course of the last few thousand years, the effect of erosion in the Hajar Mountains as a result of rainfall has brought down soil and rocks that now cover the coastal plains of the East Coast to a depth of several metres. As a result, many early archaeological sites are likely to be hidden. Certainly some have come to light only as a result of recent construction work.

One such is a tomb from the Wadi Suq period, which lasted from around 2000 BC to 1300 BC. Although the tomb itself, in the Mraishid area in the south of Fujairah City, was destroyed by the building work, artefacts from it are on display in Fujairah's Museum, close to the city's restored castle. Other concealed Wadi Suq tombs have also been found at Dhadnah, discovered during the laying of an electricity cable, and in Sharm and Dibba, and it is reasonable to assume that others may lie hidden in and around other coastal villages and towns.

Many of the tombs from this period were built on higher ground, both in mountain valleys and on the lower slopes of the mountains where they extend to the coastal plain. During the course of the last 20 years, extensive archaeological survey work has been carried out in Fujairah by teams from the local museum, as well as from Britain, Switzerland and Australia. As a result, literally hundreds of stone tombs have been discovered, dating both to the third-millennium BC and to the early second-millennium BC (the Wadi Suq period).

One such tomb is at Bithna, in Wadi Ham. On a bluff overlooking the wadi, scientists from the Swiss-Liechtenstein Foundation for Archaeological Research Abroad found scatters of pottery and soft-stone vessels on the surface as well as large stones that indicated the presence of a buried structure. Digging down, they found several graves. Most were simple circular cairns, one so small it could have been for the interment of a child.

More impressive, though, was a massive grave built of enormous stone blocks set in the earth to a height of around two metres, and shaped like a T, with the crossbar being used for a burial chamber and the portion at right angles to it being the entrance. Great stone slabs had probably covered the tomb when it was built, although these had long since been removed.

Unlike other tombs of the same period found in the Emirates, the Bithna grave had an entrance paved with large flat stones, sloping downwards to where a door had once been placed. Now fenced to ensure its preservation, the tomb has become a popu-

Man settled wherever potable water was available and a number of old wells may still be seen in Fujairah.

lar tourist attraction for visitors to Bithna.

During the Umm al-Nar period, tombs throughout the UAE appear mainly to have been of the traditional circular type first identified on the island of Umm al-Nar itself. During the Wadi Suq period, however, there was a wide range of funerary architecture, as shown by other discoveries elsewhere in Fujairah.

In the village of Sharm, just north of Bidiya, for example, a tomb resembling the Neolithic passage-graves of Western Europe has been excavated by a team from Australia's University of Sydney. Like the Bithna grave, it's built of great boulders, but is narrow and rectangular in shape, with its sides sloping in to form an arched roof.

Another tomb, in Bidiya itself, is similar to that at Sharm, but much longer, around 30 metres in length. Excavated by the Al Ain Department of Antiquities and Tourism, it yielded a number of skeletons and fragments of pottery from the early Wadi Suq period, around 1800 BC. Here, as at Bithna and Sharm, the grave appears to have been used by the local com-

The Bithna tomb, the only one of its type so far discovered in Arabia, was unearthed in 1987.

munity long after it was originally built, for material from the Iron Age (circa 1300–300 BC) and even later, was found among the remains.

Other graves from the Wadi Suq period, also dug by an Al Ain team, have been found in the village of Qidfa. Constructed in a horseshoe shape, they represent yet another variation on the tomb architecture of the second-millennium BC.

The examination of an undisturbed ancient burial ground is the dream of any archaeologist, because of the opportunity it provides to obtain information about the way of life of a now vanished people. One of the Qidfa graves provided just that. Using a bulldozer one day in 1985 to level a mound of earth that lay in the middle of his small plot of land, a farmer noticed that the machine had uncovered a hidden recess in the earth. Stopping to look, he saw scattered bones and metal implements in the soil beneath.

Halting work, he called in the local authorities, who ordered an immediate cessation of all activity until expert help could be called upon. The result, it soon became clear, was the uncovering of a rare, undisturbed tomb. Initially thought to be of an Iron Age date, this first of the Qidfa tombs to be excavated has subsequently been assigned a date in the Wadi Suq period, again around 1800 BC, although, like many

of the tombs of this period in the Emirates, it was re-used at a later date. It yielded a vast hoard of artefacts, including bronze vessels, swords, daggers, axes and bracelets, as well as a wealth of pottery.

Though many items were of kinds known from other excavations in the Emirates, some, such as two daggers with handles of wood and ivory, were the first of their type to be discovered locally. Some of the finer implements from the Qidfa grave are now on display at the Fujairah Museum.

Other graves from the Wadi Suq period have also been found amid the palm groves in Dibba, while many of the unexcavated stone mounds and cairns that line the hillsides of Fujairah are also likely to date to this time.

During this period, the closing centuries of the UAE's Bronze Age, it seems probable that the valleys and coastal plains of Fujairah were able to support a relatively large population. Although small-scale agriculture in the mountains, fishing and animal husbandry would have provided food for the inhabitants, something more would have been required to account for the existence of a society that was evidently sufficiently organised to build massive stone tombs, and to maintain them for re-use for hundreds of years. The answer may well have been the copper industry.

Throughout the mountains of Fujairah, the hill-sides are pock-marked with small holes and caves, sometimes no more than a few square metres in size. Investigations carried out by archaeologists from the University of Sydney have shown that many of these are small copper mines, the holes being left after the softer copper ore itself had been extracted. In some areas, such as a plain near Awhala, great scatters of copper slag, showing the people of Fujairah not only mined the ore but also smelted it to make tools or for export, have been found.

The copper industry of the Hajar Mountains lasted for thousands of years. Some of the older sites have provided dates in the second-millennium BC (3,000–4,000 years ago), while Carbon 14 dating of smelting sites in Wadi Hail, near Fujairah City, has yielded dates in the 17th century, more than 3,000 years later. Excavations by the University of Sydney of kilns at Ain al-Madhab, close to Fujairah itself, indicate the technical sophistication of the industry, with the kilns being able to produce heat sufficient to smelt high-quality copper for export.

Over the centuries, however, the need for fuel to fire the kilns led to a gradual denuding of the mountains as the trees were cut down. A declining pattern of rainfall also meant that it was more difficult for young trees to become established. The small size of the individual copper deposits, combined with the increasing difficulty of obtaining firewood, eventually rendered the industry uneconomic, and it faded away.

Iron Age fortresses

The Iron Age in the Emirates began around 1300 BC and lasted for a thousand years. Evidence from elsewhere in the Emirates suggests this was a period of substantial prosperity, with the country being divided into a network of little states that traded widely, while the population devised new techniques of agriculture that permitted them to flourish despite declining rainfall.

In Fujairah, at least three substantial Iron Age forts have been identified. One, at Husn Madhab, excavated by Swiss archaeologists in the late 1980s, is on a hill that overlooks the plain of Fujairah itself. Surrounded by a sturdy wall and well-fortified gateway, it appears to have been associated with a settlement on the lower slopes of the hill while, with the Ain al-Madhab copper mines nearby, it was well situated to play a role in maritime trade.

The second fort, at Awhala in the south of the emirate, lies on a wadi terrace overlooking the gorge of Wadi Qawr, a few kilometres upstream from the Batinah Coast and was restored in 2004. One side of the fort had been eroded away by the flow of the wadi, but the surviving walls, built of great boulders

The Bithna tomb features a 'dromos' entrance and shows signs of multiple use in ancient times.

and more than two-metres thick, suggested that the original enclosure was a rectangular structure of at least 50 metres by 50 metres. It was excavated in the mid-1990s by a team from the University of Sydney whose leader, Professor Dan Potts, has suggested that it may have been the capital of one of the 'Kings of Magan' referred to in the ancient Babylonian chronicles. Certainly Awhala would have been of some importance, sufficiently far from the sea to offer protection from maritime attack, yet commanding the major Wadi Qawr trade route that traversed the Hajar Mountains to the Arabian Gulf coast.

Traces of other forts can be seen in wadis and on strategically placed hilltops throughout the emirate, as in Wadi Saham and overlooking the mouth of Wadi Safad. Although many have not yet been investigated by archaeologists, some may also date to the Iron Age, or may be the remains of Islamic forts which, like the one at Awhala, rest on Iron Age foundations. Certainly the whole of Fujairah was occupied in Iron Age times, for a cemetery from the period has been partly excavated in Bidiya, while Iron Age pottery and other artefacts have been found in tombs in Qidfa, Bidiya, Sharm, Dibba and Bithna that were first constructed during the earlier Wadi Suq period.

In early 2002, excavations by a French team of a site in Bithna first identified by a Swiss team several years earlier uncovered the remains of a small building with internal pillars decorated with snake motifs. This has been interpreted as an Iron Age temple. On a hilltop nearby, a fort covering an area of some 8,000 square metres, again dated to the Iron Age, was also discovered. Within it was a black rock with a flattish surface of approximately three square metres, decorated with engravings of camels, plant leaves and examples of an early script as yet undeciphered.

Although a considerable amount of archaeological work has taken place in Fujairah during the last couple of decades, the profusion of ancient sites is such that only a tiny proportion of them have been examined. By chance, some of the sites that have been excavated date to the period from the end of the Iron Age until the coming of Islam in the early seventh-century AD, although there's no doubt that, once again, there was widespread settlement in Fujairah during this period.

Tantalising glimpses of a relatively sophisticated lifestyle, involving trading connections with other countries throughout the region, have been gained from discoveries of burials from this period inside older tombs, as at Bithna and Bidiya, and from other finds, as yet not fully studied, from Dibba. Research elsewhere – as well as careful study of historical manuscripts – has shown that around 2,000 years ago, sailors from Dibba were crossing the Indian Ocean as far as China, impressive testimony to the maritime skills of the people of Fujairah.

Aerial photographs of Dibba show that the town was once much larger than it is today, stretching across the fertile plain, while fragments of pottery collected from the surface also testify to links with India and Sri Lanka. Part of a state ruled by the Al Julanda family, Dibba was the site of a major regional

An early Islamic graveyard at Dibba, a burial ground for 10,000 slain warriors.

market and, at one period before the coming of Islam, was even the capital of the whole of Oman and south-eastern Arabia.

In the early seventh-century AD, news came of a new religion in Western Asia with the revelation of Islam to the Prophet Mohammed (PBUH). In the ninth year of the new Muslim era, 630 AD, one of the great Muslim generals, Amr ibn al-As, arrived in eastern Arabia with letters from the Prophet, seeking adherents to the new faith. He found a ready response from the Al Julanda, who were eager to throw off the yoke of the Sasanian Emperors who then controlled much of the coastline. Swiftly, the people rallied to the new religion.

After the death of the Prophet, however, a local dignitary, Dhul Taj Lakit bin Malik, sought to win power for himself and rebelled. The Al Julanda collected their forces while the Prophet's successor, the Caliph Abu Bakr, sent armies of his own across the peninsula to aid them in quelling the uprising. During a great battle just outside Dibba, the Muslim forces finally won the day. Known in Muslim history as 'The Day of Dibba', it's said some 10,000 people were slain. Their graves can still be seen in a large graveyard outside the town, just across the border in the Sultanate of Oman. The town itself was sacked, and entered a decline that lasted for several centuries.

Evidence of the Islamic history of Fujairah can still be traced in every village and on almost every hillside throughout the emirate. Small graveyards and little stone watch-towers are everywhere, while many of the terraced fields that can be seen along the sides of the wadis probably date back to the early Islamic period. More impressive are the stronger forts and fortresses, of which those at Fujairah itself and at Bithna are the best known, though others can be found in places such as Safad, Awhala and Maidaq, mute evidence of the conflicts that flowed back and forth through the mountains.

Occupation continued, too, along the coastal strip. During preparatory work for the desalination and power plant at Qidfa, in early 2002, mid-Islamic pottery was identified on now-abandoned fields between today's date-palm gardens and the coast suggesting that, several hundred years ago, the village might have occupied a larger area than it does today.

Drawings in the Portuguese colonial archives in Lisbon show the ground plans of forts that they built along the coast. The largest was at Dibba. A surviving description of the way it looked in 1646 gives an idea of how impressive it must have been.

"It is built in the shape of a square with four round bas-

A pendant of electrum from the Bidiya tomb. Artefacts from the tomb date back to at least 1000 BC.

tions in the corners and an artillery tower in the middle with a well. Each wall is seven bracas long and four in length and eleven palmos in width. It is made of stone and has parapets. Inside the fortress, there is a house for the Captain, a Church and an underground warehouse for ammunition; there are hollow spaces among the bastions for storing provisions. As well as this, the fortress has an outer fence which is very long, and is built in the shape of a square with five bastions, one of them over the gate and the other four in the corners. The gate is used as a guard's quarters. . . . There are houses for the soldiers inside the enclosure."

It must have been an imposing structure, although no trace of it remains, and even its location has been forgotten – one of the mysteries of the emirate's archaeology. A much smaller fort was situated at Bidiya, and was excavated by an Australian team in the late 1990s.

The large surviving fortresses at Fujairah itself and at Bithna, like the fort at Awhala, were probably built in the late 17th or early 18th centuries, after the Portuguese were driven out of the area, as were many other small hilltop forts, such as those in Wadi Safad and at Qurrayah.

However barren parts of Fujairah may seem today, it is increasingly clear from the archaeological record that the area flourished in the distant past with, until recent times, a continuing heritage of careful exploitation of the available natural resources on land and involvement in maritime trade that stretched far and wide around the Indian Ocean. As the process of archaeological study develops, yet more of the emirate's history will come to light.

For visitors today some of the key sites, such as those at Bithna and Bidiya, are carefully protected and displayed, while the recently upgraded Fujairah Museum provides a useful introduction to several of the most impressive finds.

Chapter six

Bullfights and boating

THE EMIRATE OF FUJAIRAH, IN COMMON WITH OTHER parts of the UAE's East Coast and the rest of the Hajar Mountains, has a heritage and a fauna and flora that is distinctly different from other parts of the United Arab Emirates, largely because of the terrain and its location on the shores of the Indian Ocean.

Elsewhere in the UAE, the camel and the falcon play a major role in local customs and tradition; the first as a beast of burden, a source of food and a racing animal, and the latter as a bird used in the popular sport of falconry, once a useful way of providing a supplement to an otherwise restricted diet. Neither is commonly found in Fujairah.

The stony terrain of the East Coast and the mountains does not lend itself to the camel, a desert beast whose feet are better adapted to the sandy plains of the Arabian Gulf coast. For the people of the mountains, who were settled in their rocky wadis, and not nomadic like the Bedouin, a camel was of little use as a working animal, donkeys being better able to pick their way through the boulders and over the

Fujairah's national sport of bullfighting is unknown elsewhere in the UAE.

hillsides. Thus, although camels can be seen in the Emirate of Fujairah, primarily on the western side of the mountains near Habhab, it's the only one of the seven emirates that today lacks its own purpose-built camel racetrack.

Similarly, the sport of falconry is little known here. The vastly different geography has an effect upon local wildlife. The Houbara Bustard, favoured quarry of falconers in the past, migrates to and from deserts, not mountains.

Instead, from its heritage of small-scale agriculture watered by carefully built channels and wells that tap into the underground water resources, Fujairah has developed its own unique sport – bullfighting. No Spanish-style *corrida* this: there are no matadors or picadors, no sword-wielding or splendidly garbed men defying death and swirling their capes, looking for the chance to deliver a thrust to the bull's spinal cord.

The contest pits not man against bull, but bull against bull, great pampered beasts weighing a ton or more, and carefully bred from the humped Brahmin cattle that can still, on occasion, be seen working the odd water wheel in Fujairah's palm groves, although of course they have now largely been replaced by diesel-powered pumps.

Raised on a diet of milk, honey and meal, the prize bulls are valued for the massiveness of their necks and shoulders and the sturdiness of their haunches. The Fujairah sport is bloodless, a contest of stolid strength. The beasts, cautiously led into a makeshift arena with two ropes tied around their necks, lower their heads, lock horns and wrestle to see which one can force the other to the ground, or make him turn tail and flee. The horns are blunt, and there's little or no side-swiping of an opponent's flanks.

Every weekend during the winter months, crowds gather in Fujairah and neighbouring towns to see the bulls engaged head to head in clouds of dust, urging on their favourites and booing their opponents. Although there's no blood, and the bulls occasionally need to be encouraged to get on with the contest at hand, rather than idly graze on a pile of hay, that's not to say there's no excitement.

From time to time, an imaginative bull will decide that his opponent really is not worth bothering about, and will make a break for freedom, charging across the ring pulling his handlers behind him in a cloud of dust. The bull will approach the circled spectators, more to find a way out than to attack them, but nevertheless

Handlers encourage their beasts in a contest where bulls are pitted against other bulls and not man.

scattering them in all directions. Eventually, the bull will lose interest and settle down, perhaps chewing comfortably on a mouthful of grass, while admiring children come to pat him on his huge flanks.

One tradition says the sport was introduced to the East Coast during the time of the Portuguese, in the 16th and 17th centuries. Interestingly, an almost identical sport exists in parts of western India formerly ruled by the Portuguese and there, too, local tradition has it that the sport was imported. Some Fujairah people, however, say the sport pre-dates the arrival of Islam in the Emirates, and suggest it may even represent an echo of that time, before the coming of Islam when the bull was an object of worship in south-western Arabia.

Certainly bulls of a similar type to those seen today are depicted on petroglyphs (rock carvings) in the mountains that are believed to date back to the Iron Age, 2,300 to 3,300 years ago.

Shashas *and shanties*

Bullfighting is a sport of the coastal plains. Besides agriculture, the coastal inhabitants of Fujairah were also intrepid fishermen, braving the breakers along the shore to venture out to the fish-filled waters beyond. Unique to this coast of the Emirates is the *shasha*, a small boat made of palm fronds bound together, that floats from the buoyancy of the material from which it is constructed – at least for a few voyages until it gets waterlogged. One local family still retains the skills to make *shashas* in the traditional way, and the craft can be seen on the coast at Fujairah or Qurrayah, pulled up on the sands.

While most fishermen have now moved over to petrol-driven fibreglass boats, they still go out with their long nets to drive the sardine shoals close inshore, from where they can be pulled on to the beach. Visitors with an eye for a good photograph, or those wishing to record the sounds of local sea shanties, in a rollicking rhythm and an almost impenetrable dialect, will find that the harvesting of the sea provides a good opportunity to savour the traditional life of Fujairah's inshore fishermen, even if many of those engaged in the industry are now temporary expatriate workers.

Up in the Hajar Mountains above Dibba, the Shihuh tribe, cousins of the Sharqiyyin, can be found. Visitors venturing high in the mountains may come across their stone-built villages, camouflaged against the rock and with a few tiny pockets of agriculture to supplement their livestock. They will most often be encountered, though, down in the town, where those that continue to hold fast to their traditions can easily be distinguished by their trademark – an axe with a small head, almost like an American Indian tomahawk, set on a long handle that is often decoratively carved and bound with silver bands. The

Rich in protein, small fish such as these are frequently dried in the sun and used for food, fodder and fertiliser.

Shihuh are now becoming aware of, and affected by, the burgeoning tourist industry and the lucky visitor may find the opportunity to bargain for one of these beautiful little weapons.

Caution should be taken when venturing into the mountains, and not only because of the roughness of the terrain. A village that appears deserted may just have been temporarily vacated during the week, or during the height of summer. Owners do not look kindly upon anyone trying to remove an attractive carved door, or carry away a large traditional pot. In the mountains, too, water is always in short supply, even today, when piped supplies reach all but the tiniest of settlements, and the local inhabitants are never pleased if strangers are seen to be wasting supplies or tampering with their water-collection systems.

Similarly, the dried-up mud channels in the mountain wadis or the coastal plains may simply be dry because of drought, or because a few days have passed since the last rush of water was let loose to irrigate the trees. The walls of the channels should be stepped over, not trodden upon, while the positioning of a few stones blocking a channel is carefully done to ensure that the water goes precisely where the farmer intends. They should not be moved. Such channels have made

The Sooty Gull, with its distinctive long bill, is found only between the Arabian Gulf and the Gulf of Suez.

Terns, gulls and other seabirds are often found near fishermen, especially when pulling in their nets.

Shashas (traditional small craft made from palm fronds) are still made and can be seen on the coast at Fujairah.

Fishing boats in the picturesque harbour near Bidiya, scenically situated against the Hajar Mountains.

it possible for the people of Fujairah to survive for thousands of years. They represent an important, if fragile, part of the emirate's heritage.

The sensitive visitor who takes care not to damage the palm groves, nor to camp amid the collection of upright stones that mark a Muslim graveyard, will find that wandering around the older villages and their agricultural plots will provide a glimpse of life in times gone by. Such villages can be found throughout the mountain areas and for some, now approached by tarmac roads, there's no need for a 4x4.

Even along the coast, visitors who venture along the dusty tracks between the palm groves will find well-kept examples of traditional gardens, such as those in the heart of Fujairah City itself, just beneath the castle.

Bulls are now rarely to be seen groaning as they pull water up a long incline, the put-put of a diesel engine now being more usual, but there may still be a young lad shinning up a palm trunk without visible means of support to slice off a ripe bunch of dates. Or, dozing quietly on the hillside in the shade of a bush, a shepherd may be keeping half an eye on his flock of grazing goats and sheep.

Variety in wildlife

In the middle of all this, at the top of the mountains or in a deep wadi, in a coastal palm grove or a fertile

Each day, thousands of small fish are loaded onto small trucks near Fujairah.

Nature's arid garden rockery: a colourful, harmonious display in a quiet corner of Wadi Wurrayah.

Rain clouds over Wadi Hail.

field, there's always the chance of catching a glimpse of some of Fujairah's flora and fauna. After rainfall, the mountains blossom not only with lush green grass, but with a blaze of colour from tiny plants that hurry to sprout, flower and seed before the last remnants of moisture dry up. Among the flowers, the lucky observer may find the delicate bloom of one of Arabia's few species of orchids, a hardy survivor from a time when there was more rainfall.

Nimbly picking its way across a hillside, there may be an Arabian gazelle, although the caracal or lynx, the Arabian tahr (a relative of the goat) and, most rare of all, the highly endangered Arabian leopard, are more wary of people and seen by only the most fortunate.

The little pools of perennial water in the wadis hold several species of freshwater fish as well as toads, whose croaking is sometimes the only sound to be heard in the

Dates were an important staple in the diet of the people of the Emirates before the arrival of oil wealth.

more remote areas. Brilliantly coloured dragonflies can be found here too, as well as butterflies, while snakes such as the harmless wadi racer may be seen slipping in and out of the water in search of prey.

Along the coast, and up in the mountains too, the East Coast of the UAE is home to a remarkable variety of migrant and resident birds. More than 300 species have been recorded in the area, with new additions being ticked every year. Some can be seen nowhere else in the region, and the East Coast has won recognition among local and foreign bird-watchers as one of the prime birding destinations in the region.

Even for the utter novice, the brilliant blue wings of an Indian Roller or the shimmering plumage of a Purple Sunbird provide stunning flashes of colour amid the vegetation, while the sight of hundreds of gulls and terns swooping and diving above a shoal of fish just offshore, or a pair of Bonelli's eagles in a courting display, soaring above the mountains, takes a lot of beating.

Prime spots for bird-watching are the well-wooded pools at Qurrayah, just north of Fujairah City; the Wadi Zikt reservoir, a haunt of migrant grebe and ducks during the winter months; and the extensive fodder fields at the Fujairah National Dairy Farm at Dibba, hard up against the border with Oman, although good birding can be enjoyed almost anywhere.

Close to the beaches, turtles can sometimes be seen. A few are believed to still nest on the beach at Khor Kalba, south of Fujairah.

Further offshore, for those able to take boat trips out to sea, not only is the sport-fishing magnificent, but there's the chance to see frolicking schools of dolphins and, even further from the coast and less frequently, the occasional great whale as it breaches the water's surface, jumping high and re-

A solitary watch-tower stands guard over a verdant palm grove, scenically situated at Maydaq, near Masafi.

The East Coast is recognised as one of the prime bird-watching destinations in the region.

entering the ocean with a resounding splash.

The beaches themselves hold treasures too, fragments of delicate coral and a remarkable variety of seashells, some much sought after by collectors. Three species of seashell were first discovered on the beach at Qurrayah, and are not known from anywhere except the East Coast.

At the request of Fujairah's ruler, their Latin scientific names were derived from those of three nearby villages, Mirbah, Safad and Girath, to com-

memorate the traditional links between the people of Fujairah and the sea.

Throughout Fujairah, the unique customs and traditions of the people and the startling variety of plant and animal life can be found in a terrain that's far removed from the conceptions, or misconceptions, of what makes up the Arabian Peninsula. The Fujairah coastline, and the mountains that lie behind it, are attractive precisely because they are so different – and therein lies much of the charm of this emirate.

Flowers grow even in the arid parts of the mountains.

Toads are common and noisy residents of the wadis.

Chapter seven

Developing the economy

A SIMPLE GLANCE AT THE SCENERY OF THE EMIRATE of Fujairah shows that its appearance is markedly different from that of the other emirates. Dominated by mountains, rather than plains and deserts, its geology is entirely different, and that applies just as much under the surface as above. Great folds in the rocks, caused by cataclysmic earth movements, have meant that none of the 'traps' that hold large quantities of oil and gas reserves elsewhere in the country have so far been identified.

While oil exploration continues, the Government of Fujairah recognises that its economy is never likely to be able to depend purely on oil as a source of revenue.

Fortunately, however, the benefits of geology and geography are not confined to oil wealth. Instead, Fujairah's location and its rugged mountains offer opportunities of a different kind – opportunities that

Agriculture is a traditional mainstay of the local economy, with the surplus sold outside the emirate.

The Friday Market near Masafi is a favourite destination for Nationals, expatriates and even tourists.

have permitted the development of a widely diversified economy and one in which, moreover, oil does play an important part.

Just like the rest of the UAE, Fujairah has, of course, benefited from the investment in the infrastructure made by the Federal Government in schools, hospitals, power plants and other services.

Perhaps one of the most important pieces of this federal investment in infrastructure as far as Fujairah has been concerned is the building of the great road that winds across the mountains from Dhaid to Masafi, and then down Wadi Ham to the sea at Fujairah itself. Completed only in the late 1970s and recently upgraded, it gave the emirate its first all-weather access to the rest of the country.

Since then, Fujairah's economy has developed steadily, if quietly and undramatically, and it is now firmly established as one of the fastest-growing non-oil sectors of the UAE economy.

Top government officials, such as Sheikh Saleh bin Mohammed Al Sharqi, younger brother of the emirate's ruler and Chairman of the Department of Economy and Industry, stress that the long-term

planning for Fujairah's future rests upon the need to develop a variety of sources of income. Agriculture, light industry, shipping, trade and tourism have all attracted considerable attention and, in all of these fields, Fujairah has seen remarkable growth, particularly during the last decade.

The objective behind the emirate's development planning, according to Sheikh Saleh, has been "to utilise and develop all its resources and potential, to create an integrated and strong economy that will be able to survive any sudden fluctuations in any sector."

As has happened in the other emirates, Fujairah has not neglected the possibility of finding oil and gas reserves. The complicated local geology, however, coupled with the water depths of the offshore Gulf of Oman – much deeper than in the Arabian Gulf – have meant that Fujairah has, thus far, failed to join the ranks of the UAE's oil producers.

Although an exploration well in the Bay of Dibba early in 1989 proved unsuccessful, the development of technology permitting exploration in the deeper waters offshore has ensured oil companies continue to display an interest in Fujairah. In early 2005, a new oil concession agreement for the whole of the emirate, covering both offshore and onshore areas, was awarded to a consortium of Naftogaz, of Ukraine, and Abu Dhabi-based Al Jazirah.

Despite the lack of success to date in oil and gas exploration, Fujairah's economy is, nonetheless, now heavily dependent on oil, though on the downstream rather than the upstream part of the industry, thanks to the good fortune of its location.

"Making use of our geographic location is a key part of our development strategy," says Fujairah's Ruler, Sheikh Hamad, and one of the greatest industrial success stories of the UAE has been the dramatic emergence of Fujairah as a transport hub for the region, in which the port, the airport, the free zone and

the supply of bunker oil to shipping have all played their part.

Lying on the shores of the Gulf of Oman, and near to the strategic Strait of Hormuz, the Fujairah coastline is ideally situated close to the key shipping routes of the Indian Ocean and can be reached without an expensive, and sometimes dangerous, detour into the nearly land-locked Arabian Gulf.

The completion of the road through the Hajar Mountains came at precisely the time when the Government of Fujairah was beginning to look at ways of diversifying its traditional economy. With the outbreak of the Iraq-Iran War in 1980, major shipping lines began looking at alternative ways of shipping goods into the Arabian Gulf, and the opening of the

The Port of Fujairah is ideally situated close to major international shipping routes.

Containers being offloaded at Fujairah, which has emerged as one of the world's top-40 container ports.

Port of Fujairah in 1982 provided them with an ideal way of avoiding the zone of conflict.

High insurance rates for shipping inside the Arabian Gulf prompted many ship owners to keep their vessels safely outside. Fujairah's port was quick to benefit not only from providing services for the rapidly expanding container business but also from the supply of fuel and other goods to vessels making use of the safe anchorage just offshore.

In recent years, the supply of bunker fuel has

Fujairah's refinery and oil storage tanks, with the Hajar Mountains in the background.

prompted the setting up not only of an oil refinery, now partly owned by the Fujairah Government, but also the establishment of oil-tank farms. The largest of these, VOPAK Emirates, is also partly government-owned, with a third phase of expansion under way. When it is completed, nearly Dhs 680 million will have been invested in the project.

Fujairah is now the second-largest bunkering centre in the world, having overtaken Rotterdam, and only Singapore is larger.

In 2002, 11.5 million tons of fuel were handled through Fujairah, serving more than 6,000 ships and, although the total fell back in 2003 because of conflict in the region, the 2004 trend showed a return to expansion in this sector. At any one time, up to 100 vessels can be seen anchored offshore.

In a move to reduce the amount of marine pollution offshore, which can wash onto Fujairah's beaches, the government is seeking to phase out the anchorage of oil-storage vessels offshore and to ensure that the demand for bunker fuel is, in future, supplied wholly from onshore tank farms.

The latest project on the drawing board is the building of an oil pipeline from Abu Dhabi to Fujairah, so that oil production from the UAE's largest producer is no longer subject to the vicissitudes of the stormy waters of Gulf politics. The likely terminal is close to the existing oil refinery, north of the Port of Fujairah, although an expansion of that refinery, or the building of a new one, is likely to be necessary in the near future. Much of the route of the new pipeline has already been prepared, thanks to the laying of water and gas pipelines through the mountains to the power and desalination plant at Qidfa. When the new oil pipeline is complete, even though Fujairah has no oil of its own, it will enjoy an economy very much related to oil.

The Port of Fujairah has itself grown over the years even though, like all other ports, it is affected by the changing patterns of the global shipping industry.

The Fujairah Free Zone has helped to contribute to the development of the air-sea freight business.

During 2002, for example, improved port facilities in Bombay (Mumbai) meant that one of the major container lines that formerly used Fujairah as a transhipment point reduced its number of calls. Despite this, the total tonnage passing through Fujairah still rose by some 4.5 per cent over the previous year, to nearly 21-million tons.

A flexible operations and marketing strategy continues to seek out new business, while the steady growth in the number of vessels calling at the port, which reached 1,957 ships in 2003, is handled through a continuing programme of expanding quay space and deepening the basins and approaches. Container handling capacity will soon reach one-million TEUs a year. A major new expansion programme at the port, due to be completed by early 2005, will add an additional 820-metre quay, capable of accommodating two vessels of up to 180,000 dwt. Associated shore-bunkering facilities will make it possible for the phasing out of the moored bunkering tankers offshore, with associated cost and environmental benefits.

The services offered by the port have been augmented by those of Fujairah International Airport, which opened in 1987. Although used mainly by re-

gional, rather than global carriers, as well as by charter operators, it too has recorded steady growth, helped by the fact that it is both the only international airport on the UAE East Coast and also serves the whole of northern Oman. During 2003, passenger traffic rose by 56 per cent over the previous year, which had itself seen a two-thirds increase over the 2001 figure, while aircraft movements in 2003 were 41 per cent higher than in 2002.

The airport was expanded in 2004 to give it a new look, to provide it with more modern facilities and to ensure more comfort, accessibility and efficiency for passengers. A new terminal is planned for the next stage of development.

The success of the port and airport helped to prompt the establishment of the Fujairah Free Zone, which began operations early in 1992. Located adjacent to the port, and a few minutes' drive from the airport, the zone has helped to contribute to the development of the air-sea freight business, and has also attracted substantial investment.

Wary of depending too heavily on a single type of product, the Free Zone Authority, headed by Sheikh Saif bin Hamad, son of Fujairah's Deputy Ruler, has

Investment in agricultural infrastructure has included the building of reservoirs in mountain wadis.

made a point of seeking to attract a variety of customers. These include garment manufacturers, as well as a host of other companies making a variety of high-tech, packaging and other products. By the end of 2003 more than 320 companies from more than 25 countries around the globe had been established in the zone, with nearly Dhs 1.5 billion invested in it. In excess of 4,250 people work in the zone, which represents a major source of employment in the emirate.

The zone covers an area of 500,000 square metres, with further expansion being planned. Growth of investment in the zone has averaged more than 21 per cent annually in recent years with success being achieved not only in attracting manufacturing companies but also trading offices. The low-cost operations are certainly attractive to firms wishing to test the UAE's economic waters before deciding to commit themselves to heavy capital investment.

While the airport, port, free zone and oil-related installations stretching northwards along the coast towards the village of Qurrayah are perhaps the most visible signs of Fujairah's burgeoning industrial economy, there are other important components as well.

One is the major desalination and water-generation plant at Qidfa, some 20 kilometres north of Fujairah, hidden away on the shore behind flourishing palm gardens. This project, built by the Union Water and Electricity Company (UWEC) under the aegis of the Abu Dhabi-based UAE Offsets Programme, is the largest reverse-osmosis desalination plant in the world. Its initial phase, completed in 2004, produces 656 MW of power a day, and 100-million gallons of water a day, and cost some Dhs 2.94 billion. Work on a second plant commenced in 2004, with completion scheduled for the middle of 2008. This will increase capacity by up to 1,000 MW of power and another 100-million gallons a day of water.

The new Qidfa plant will not only supply Fujairah with all its water and power for many years to come, but will also become the main hub of an electricity-generation network for the whole of the Northern Emirates, and may eventually export power to several neighbouring countries through the planned GCC power grid.

Much of the desalinated water is destined for Abu Dhabi's inland oasis city of Al Ain, to permit further development of its cultivated areas, although water is also sent by pipeline to Dhaid, in the Emirate of

Sharjah, for distribution throughout the Northern Emirates. Fuel for the plant is being supplied by Abu Dhabi-based Dolphin Energy, which is sending gas bought from Oman through another parallel pipeline from Al Ain to Qidfa. Once this gas is depleted, Dolphin will supply gas from Qatar.

Another major project, announced in mid-2004, is a steel plant, to be built near Fujairah's port, which will be financed by the Abu Dhabi Investment Company (ADIC). When completed, it will have a capacity of 1.2-million tons of steel a year, along with a steel-billet production line and a sponge iron unit. With the necessary raw materials being imported by sea, the plant will not only provide a further boost to Fujairah's own industrial economy but will also generate substantial new business for the port.

The steel plant, along with the already operating oil refinery and oil-tank farm, will provide the core of Fujairah's expanding industrial economy – and much of the area north of the port and south of the next coastal village, Qurrayah, has already been allocated by the government for further industrial ventures.

While projects such as these represent the major components of Fujairah's industrial economy today, they are of relatively recent origin.

Also of importance are a number of industries that began a little earlier, many of them based on the exploitation of the natural resources of the emirate itself. Thus the rocks of the mountains have been utilised as raw material by makers of aggregates (as at Wadi Saqamqam), of cement (as at Dibba) and for marble tiles (near Fujairah City), while large boulders from the mountains now make up much of the coastal defence and breakwaters of the cities of the UAE's Arabian Gulf coast.

The copper-mining industry that first began in Fujairah's mountains more than 5,000 years ago finally died away in the 16th or 17th century with the exhaustion of ore deposits, but other commercially viable deposits of minerals have taken its place. One such deposit was of many thousands of tons of chromite ore in a tributary of Wadi Hail, just outside Fujairah City, which was mined for several years in the 1990s before it too was exhausted.

Further expansion of the mining industry is unlikely to be very significant, however, not only because a

Agriculture thrives in the wadis, where farmers take full advantage of traditional irrigation practices.

Fresh fruit and vegetables at the Friday Market.

lack of commercially viable deposits, but also because Fujairah's Ruler, Sheikh Hamad, is concerned about the adverse impact upon the emirate's mountain environment – and that is of major significance for another fast-growing sector of the economy, tourism.

All of the development began, though, with the growth of existing traditional economic sectors in the early years of the UAE Federation.

"The people of Fujairah have always been farmers and fishermen," says the Ruler, Sheikh Hamad, who goes on to note that, as a result, "we have devoted considerable investment to the agriculture and fisheries sector."

The underground water resources in the mountains, whether captured by small canals in the wadis or used where those wadis debouch on to the coastal plains, have permitted small farms to flourish, while the well-stocked waters of the Gulf of Oman provide fishermen with food for local consumption throughout the year.

Exporters of food

Before the establishment of the UAE, the people of Fujairah were primarily concerned with producing enough food for their own consumption. Today, however, thanks to the all-weather road link to the

Testing the date harvest.

Fine blossoms at the Siji Greenhouse Company, where flowers are grown for export to Europe.

rest of the country, local farmers in the mountains and on the coast of the Gulf of Oman can join their fellow Fujairans on the western side of the mountains, in areas such as Habhab and Siji, in aspiring, not only to grow enough food for Fujairah's own growing population, but also to produce a marked surplus to sell in the several hungry markets of the cities on the Arabian Gulf coast.

Fujairah's geography, with its high mountains, and climate – with more rainfall, particularly in the mountains, than most of the rest of the Emirates – permits its farmers to grow a wider range of crops. This is particularly noticeable in terms of fruit production, with not only dates, but also mangoes, papaya and a variety of citrus fruit, including limes, lemons, grapefruit and oranges, being successfully grown, often in small mountain farms, fed by traditional *falaj* water channels. Fujairah is also the UAE's principal producer of tobacco.

The basic aim of the agricultural development programme has been to achieve self-sufficiency in fruit and vegetables, and this has now largely been achieved, with a surplus in the height of the season to sell outside the emirate.

The expansion in production has been achieved partly as a result of the provision of advice and expertise to local farmers, so that they can achieve higher yields from their small fields. With the assistance of the Ministry of Agriculture and Fisheries, improved strains of plants have also been introduced, along with the use of modern fertilisers and pest-control methods.

On the coastal strip, where a larger proportion of the land is suitable for agriculture, the old method of irrigating the fields and date-palm groves by using a pulley to turn a water wheel has fallen into disuse, being replaced by pumps which can draw up the sub-surface water more quickly and efficiently. At the same time, however, with the government aware of the need to use the limited water supplies cautiously, not only have farmers been encouraged to use less-wasteful forms of irrigation, but dams have also been built to hold back the rainwater and allow it to recharge the subterranean aquifers instead of rushing uselessly into the sea or the desert.

The largest dam, in Wadi Ham just outside the city of Fujairah, has the capacity to hold several-million gallons of rainwater, while several others have been

Fruit-bearing date palms flourish at Bithna.

built, such as those in Wadi Safad and in Wadi Zikt, near Dhadnah, and at Tawiyeen, on the western side of the Hajar Mountains between Idhn and Khatt. Much smaller dams have been built by farmers throughout the mountains, often with traditional materials, to help develop their own farms.

Evidence of the emirate's thriving traditional agriculture can be seen in the markets in every town, and also along the roadsides, such as in Bidiya, or at the popular 'Friday Market' outside Masafi, where the farmers come to sell their produce – at prices much cheaper than in the supermarkets.

One result of the government's provision of support for traditional agriculture has been the continued cultivation of the small plots and fields in the mountain wadis. This in turn has helped to ensure that the people retain their links with the land.

Thus even in the remotest mountain fastnesses, farmers are able to make a living, much as their ancestors have done for hundreds of years. Nearly 2,900 small farms throughout the emirate, covering a total area of more than 52,000 *dunums*, continue to provide much of Fujairah's food.

Agri-business

While traditional farming techniques have been improved and updated, both the government and the private sector have invested in larger-scale projects.

The Department of Economy and Industry's Fujairah National Dairy Farm, near Dibba, runs a herd of around 500 head of cattle, producing milk and meat for the local market. Nearby is a research station of the federal Ministry of Agriculture and Fisheries, which also offers extension services to local farmers.

Other large agricultural enterprises include the Fujairah Farm at Dhadnah which, with the objective of creating an integrated agri-business enterprise, produces on an area of 400 hectares meat, milk, dairy products, fruit and vegetables for the local market. It has also ventured downstream into the supply of fruit juices and, using its own equipment, produces specially coated fencing wire for the local market.

Overall, Fujairah's recorded agricultural production rose from 56,400 tons in 2002 to 99,100 tons in 2003, an indication of the way in which this sector of the economy is thriving – and these figures, moreover, were recorded in years when there was relatively little winter rainfall.

Even while trapped in a net, these opportunistic fish were busy preying on smaller fish.

Another Department of Economy and Industry project is the Arab Company for Poultry Production, a joint venture between the Fujairah Government and foreign investors. There is also another, privately owned poultry farm, with the total production of both farms amounting to 14-million eggs and more than 4,100 tons of meat a year. Yet another department project is a joint venture producing supplies of equipment for farmers, all part of a programme of tailoring local industrial development to local needs.

One of the most remarkable success stories has been the Siji Greenhouse Company, on the west side of the mountains just off the main road, where the department has established more than 40,000 square metres of environmentally controlled greenhouses.

Initially specialising in the growing of vegetables, the company has now diversified into the production of flowers and has proved its quality by gaining a healthy foothold for exports to the established, lucrative flower markets of Europe.

Untapped fishing grounds

Just as local agriculture has developed in recent years, so too has there been progress in the local fishing industry. The waters of the Gulf of Oman are among the last great untapped fishing grounds in the world and, with 200 kilometres of the UAE's Exclusive Economic Zone at its disposal, the government is keen to encourage local fishermen to make the best of the opportunities on their doorsteps.

Special harbours have been built for local fisher-men at Dibba, Dhadnah, Mirbah and Fujairah, from where hundreds of small craft set out to harvest the sea – providing a good source of photographs for visitors as they unload their catch on their return. Much of the catch is of the fish to be found close inshore, caught by line or in simple pots and nets. Indeed, in some seasons of the year, shoals of sardines can even be caught off the beach and dried on the shore nearby.

Other fishermen venture further offshore, how-ever, seeking game fish such as yellow-fin tuna, which is always popular among consumers.

With an almost inexhaustible local demand for fresh fish, the government hopes to encourage foreign investors to share in the development of a deep-sea fishing industry.

Already, thanks to grants and loans on easy terms from the Ministry of Agriculture and Fisheries, Fujairah's fishing boats are better equipped, while the Department of Economy and Industry has longer-term plans to build cold stores and processing and freezing plants to further stimulate the economy.

There is, though, a recognition that it is important to ensure that the amount of fishing does not have an adverse impact on stocks. In association with the Ministry of Agriculture and Fisheries, new rules have been introduced on the types of net that can be used, and the number of licensed fishing boats has declined in recent years. The UAE Navy, too, keeps a close watch on foreign fishing vessels trying to work in Fujairah's waters.

In the long run, the future may lie, to a large extent at least, in commercial fish farming. In this sector, the initiative has been taken by the Asmak fish farm at Dibba, a project supported by the UAE Offsets Pro-gramme. With an area of more than 200,000 square metres allocated to it by the Fujairah Government, Asmak's operations include a state-of-the-art hatch-ery capable of producing 10-million juvenile fish a year, with plans for the development of a processing and packaging plant capable of handling 2,500 tons of fish annually.

'Business-friendly atmosphere'

The emirate's strategy of economic development does not seek merely to encourage foreign firms to take advantage of its geographical location as a trans-shipment base, or as a place that can provide a jumping-off point for entry into regional and overseas markets. It also seeks to attract firms to set up in Fujairah itself, as an integral part of the UAE market, and one with facilities that can match those found anywhere else in the country.

The emirate's Ruler, Sheikh Hamad bin Moham-med Al Sharqi, is a keen advocate of the need to attract foreign business. "Fujairah offers a business-friendly environment," he notes, "where we make it as easy as we can for foreign companies to set up for business. We have the advantage of a key geographic location, of course, but on top of that Fujairah offers stability and reasonable labour costs, as well as a life-

Soccer is one of the most popular sports for Fujairah's residents and scholars.

Fujairah Women's College, on the outskirts of the city.

style and surroundings that are attractive for investors and their workforce."

And, to prove it recognises that economic growth can be helped by the provision of a satisfactory living environment for citizens and expatriates alike, the local government has not only spent considerable sums of money on enhancing leisure facilities such as the new corniche and the Ain Al Madhab health spa, but has also provided backing to other institutions such as the Fujairah Private Academy, which offers top-quality British-style education. Expatriate parents with young children need no longer send them away to boarding school and this has improved the quality of life for expatriates wishing to settle with their families in Fujairah. This, in turn, can only help to facilitate the improvement of business itself.

Naturally, there has also been significant progress for UAE Nationals in recent years too. Government officials note, with pride, that Fujairah is the only one of the UAE's seven emirates where UAE citizens are in a majority, and many of those are now playing a major role in the expanding economy. That process has been helped by the expansion of the educational opportunities on offer. Besides the private sector, Fujairah's 60 government-run schools offer education to more than 45,000 students.

The opening of Fujairah Women's College, one of the nationwide network of Higher Colleges of Technology – and of a woman's campus for the Fujairah branch of the Ajman University of Science and Technology – provides about 1,000 Fujairah girls a year with access to higher education without the need to travel far from home.

Along with the growth in education, sport has not been neglected. One of the newest projects is a Dhs 20 million tennis stadium, which incorporates six tennis courts, a multi-purpose hall and seating for 3,000 spectators. This project closely follows the formation of the Fujairah Tennis Club and has been generously supported by General Sheikh Mohammed bin Rashid Al Maktoum, Crown Prince of Dubai and UAE Minister of Defence. Importantly, the project includes a facility for training juniors from Fujairah and the surrounding regions.

The rapidly rising level of education among Fujairah's people may have only an indirect impact on the development of the economy – but it is a real impact, nonetheless.

According to Sheikh Saleh, not only the main spokesman for the emirate's economic planning but also one of its leading businessmen, "Fujairah has a great and bright future. We are completing the foundations necessary to establish Fujairah as an important industrial base, a regional trade centre and a focus for tourism. Our facilities and advantages, such as our location, the port and airport, the free zone, the Trade Centre, our modern infrastructure and, above all, the determination of the authorities and people of Fujairah, will ensure that our optimism is well-founded and that we achieve our objectives."

Chapter eight

Tourism in Fujairah

Fujairah has long been a favoured destination for a day out or a holiday weekend by residents of the other emirates, both Nationals and expatriates alike. Now, as the local tourist industry gets under way, visitors from overseas are also discovering its charms.

With its stark mountains, hidden wadis and long, clean shell-strewn beaches, the East Coast and the mountains behind it provide a variety of scenery that can be found nowhere else in the country. Its picturesque small farms and ancient forts and castles add to the attractiveness of this jewel of Arabia.

Until relatively recently, Fujairah was a well-kept secret, of which few outside the country had ever heard. Now, however, the tourist industry is one of the fastest-growing sectors of the UAE economy and, Fujairah, like the other emirates, is gaining its rightful

Above: Water-skiing off Le Meridien Beach Resort near the picturesque village of Aqqah.
Left: Yachting is popular along the coast of Fujairah.

share of the trade. Between 1998 and 2002, the number of visitors staying at its main hotels rose by 46 per cent to a little more than 84,000, while a total of 220,000 tourists visited Fujairah in 2004.

According to Sheikh Saeed bin Saeed Al Sharqi, Chairman of the Fujairah Tourism Bureau, the emirate is expected to have 3,000 hotel rooms by 2010, a 300 per cent increase on the accommodation available at the beginninng of 2005. By then, the emirate is expecting to receive more than a million tourists a year. Sustaining the momentum in 2005 were the new Rotana hotel (adjacent to Le Meridien Aqqah) and the new Dhs 1.2 billion project on the Dana Island Peninsula which will consist of two breakwaters connected to two islands. More than 300 villas and a series of restaurants will be built on the two breakwaters, while 11 hotels will be built on the coastal strip between the breakwaters.

During the winter months, the weather is almost perfect for visitors from the cooler climes of Northern Europe seeking sun, sea and sand, along with a bit of culture and heritage and, at peak periods, the hotels in Fujairah City, such as the Hilton, the Siji, the Beach Motel and the Ritz Plaza, regularly find they have difficulty in accommodating the growing demand both from businessmen and women, and holidaymakers, as well as from the crews of visiting ships.

Further up the coast, Dibba has its Holiday Resort hotel, while a few kilometres to the south, near the picturesque village of Aqqah, is Le Meridien Beach Resort, a stunning five-star hotel with 218 rooms that opened for business in early 2003 and enjoyed an 80 per cent occupancy during its first year. Nearby is the Sandy Beach Motel, offering more basic accommodation, and popular among UAE residents seeking a few days off from the pressures of life in the cities on the Arabian Gulf coast. Nearby are some of the best waters for scuba-diving anywhere in the Emirates.

Also popular among UAE residents, though not suitable for those who have to travel by plane rather than with their own vehicle, is outdoor camping, either on the beaches or in the secluded mountain wadis where the local people, if often curious, are always friendly. For foreign visitors, the delights of camping out in the open can be arranged through some of the country's better tour operators.

The bulk of foreign holidaymakers in Fujairah come from European countries such as Scandinavia, France and Germany, although some now also come from as far away as Japan and North America. Much of the trade also comes from within the UAE and from neighbouring countries in the Arabian Gulf, with numbers rising quickly as the secret of Fujairah's charms leaks out and as the number of hotel rooms, chalets and serviced apartments increases to meet demand.

Many of the overseas visitors come on organised

With a selection of coral and tropical fish, 'Snoopy Island' off Sandy Beach Motel is a popular snorkelling site.

Le Meridien Aqqah, one of Fujairah's new hotels, has become extremely popular with holidaymakers.

Reflections: The porte-cochère *at the Fujairah Hilton.*

The open-air coffee lounge at the Fujairah Hilton is a popular meeting spot for locals and tourists alike.

Dibba's popular Holiday Beach Motel offers chalet-style accommodation.

package holidays, with others coming on their own, perhaps to visit friends and relatives. As Fujairah's economy grows, there's increasing demand, too, from businessmen and women who choose to stop over for a few days of relaxation, perhaps with their spouses, at the end of a long and exhausting business trip.

Until the mid-1990s, the Government of Fujairah was reluctant to agree to major new hotel projects to supplement well-established ones such as the Hilton. The emirate's infrastructure was still being expanded, to ensure that adequate supplies of water and power were available, while a number of industrial projects were nearing completion. In 1997, though, with the infrastructure now capable of coping with more tourists, the Fujairah Tourism Bureau was established with a mandate to sell the charms of the emirate, both within the UAE and at major travel markets overseas.

Complementing this, a conference and exhibition centre was built, close to the Fujairah Trade Centre, to help to sell the emirate as a location for seminars and business conferences, not only for organisations from within the region, but also from further afield.

The Chairman of the Department of Economy and Industry, Sheikh Saleh, and his colleagues in government are, nevertheless, keen to ensure that the development of the emirate's tourist industry should not be permitted either to spoil the environment or to have an adverse effect upon the lifestyle of the people. They are determined that any hotel development

The Ritz Plaza Hotel in downtown Fujairah.

Items such as Persian carpets, gold jewellery and traditional dalla *coffee pots are all on sale in Fujairah.*

should be an asset not simply in economic but also in environmental terms, and that it should also be compatible with the emirate's own way of life.

As part of plans for the long-term development of the plain on which the city of Fujairah is situated, the government insists that any hotel scheme for the area should be accompanied by a detailed environmental study, including landscaping, with the intention of creating a zone that will be of benefit for the townspeople as well as holidaymakers. The problem is not to find investors, but rather the need to identify which of the many projects on offer is most in keeping with its surroundings.

"We welcome tourism, and think it has an important part to play in our future development," says the Ruler, Sheikh Hamad bin Mohammed Al Sharqi. "Not in the form of hundreds of thousands of people,

of course," he points out. "Fujairah is a small emirate and we do not want to be submerged. We want to maintain and preserve our heritage and traditions, and that, after all, is part of the appeal of our 'Arabian Jewel' to our visitors."

The objective is to attract tourists either for holidays that will be spent purely in the Emirates, or as part of a tour of several destinations. With the airport conveniently situated for a stopover between Europe and Asia, and those of Sharjah and Dubai not far away, such an objective is by no means impractical.

At present, however, many of Fujairah's tourists spend the bulk of their holiday in other parts of the country, perhaps popping over for a day or two to sample the delights of the East Coast. Those who take the trouble to do so find that the uniquely peaceful and relaxed atmosphere is Fujairah's greatest attraction.

Fujairah boasts numerous sandy beaches, suitable for many holiday and weekend activities.

The scenery and historical monuments, described elsewhere in this book, are part of that atmosphere: in few other parts of Arabia can such dramatic sights be seen. So too are the long, unspoilt beaches, and the fine fishing offshore.

Shopping opportunities, it should be conceded, though they are growing rapidly, are not as varied or plentiful as they are, for example, in Abu Dhabi, Dubai and Sharjah. Fujairah has none of the great shopping malls of these more developed cities, although the range of goods on display in the showrooms at the Fujairah Trade Centre and the Fujairah Plaza is by no means unimpressive.

Those who wish to find gold jewellery, Persian carpets, traditional coffee pots or a range of high-quality photographic equipment will be able to do so. The more discerning visitor will find that there are other more local items available – though not in the shops. A Shihuh axe head from the mountains makes an intriguing souvenir, provided someone can be found to sell one while, as farmers switch to more modern equipment, there is the possibility of picking up an old agricultural implement, such as the special knives used for cutting bunches of dates. The range of locally made handicrafts on sale at the Fujairah Women's Social Development Centre, just behind the Taj Mahal restaurant on Sheikh Hamad bin Abdullah Street, are both unusual and attractive, while other locally made items, including decorated pottery, can be found at Masafi's Friday Market.

As always, the custom of bargaining over the price of any item adds spice to the pleasure of making a purchase. As Fujairah's economy develops, a wider variety of goods is becoming available to satisfy those for whom shopping is a prerequisite of any holiday.

For those keen on collecting mementoes of Fujairah's wildlife, the wide range of shells cast up on the emirate's beaches – many of which can be found only in this part of the Indian Ocean – can form an attractive addition to any collection.

For other visitors, the beaches offer different attractions. A good, relaxing time is, of course, available at the beachfront hotels: the Hilton, in Fujairah, and Le Meridien and the Sandy Beach at Aqqah, while sports facilities, scuba-diving and deep-sea fishing offshore are among the more energetic pursuits on offer. So important is Fujairah's marine life, in fact, that in 1995 three marine reserves were created, at Ra's Dibba, Dhadnah and Al Aqqah, to provide a safe shelter for the colourful fish, turtles and other denizens of the deep. These spots are now carefully protected by the UAE Coastguard and, along with a number of other offshore coral reefs and rocks, are popular destinations for scuba divers.

Each winter, Fujairah also hosts a round of the World International Powerboat Championships, which brings the top drivers, and their accompanying circus of followers, to town for a few days. The races are run from the Fujairah International Marine Sports Club which has purpose-built premises on the city's corniche, complete with its own small marina.

Many of Fujairah's visitors, however, find it is the opportunity to observe the traditional lifestyle of this corner of Arabia that is among the most rewarding features of a holiday in the emirate. In no other part of Arabia, or at least those parts easily accessible to tourists, is it possible to get a real feeling for what life was like in years gone by.

The heritage visible in the castles and ancient tombs is on show in the Fujairah Museum, while the old fortress of the rulers in the centre of the coastal plain has now been restored as the centrepiece of a heritage park which will include the mud-brick houses of the old town.

Other forts at Hail, Bithna and Awhala, near Ain al-Ghammour, have been or will be restored.

The palm groves that occupy much of the coastal plain on which Fujairah lies, as well as the land adjacent to each of the coastal villages, are still being worked, complete with their irrigation channels. They provide an insight into a traditional way of life that is fresh in the memories of the local people. Life in the

A fisherman's colourful catch. The East Coast of the UAE is blessed with a great variety of fish.

Traditional handicrafts being made at Fujairah's Women's Social Development Centre.

small settlements in the mountains and the traditional fishing methods have also changed little.

One palm grove that has undergone change, however, is that at Ain al-Madhab, on the outskirts of Fujairah City. Once the private property of the ruling Al Sharqi family, it has now been thrown open as a public park and health spa, complete with chalet accommodation. Its spring, or 'ain, whose waters are laden with therapeutic minerals, is the source of water for the UAE's first proper mineral spa. The people of Fujairah have long known of the beneficial qualities of the water that is now, slowly, being discovered by foreign visitors.

Deep in the mountains, another spa is being developed at Ain al-Ghammour and its therapeutic hot springs, with a 60-room hotel and 60 chalets planned.

In the valley behind Ain al-Madhab are the remains of copper-smelting ovens that are at least 1,000 years old and, nearby, a 3,000-year-old Iron Age fort, just two of the many antiquities that will fascinate the visitor. Other evidence of the copper industry as well as other archaeological sites can be found throughout the mountains, while the little stone or mud-brick forts and watch-towers in almost every village and on

many of the hilltops provide an intriguing glimpse of times gone by, though the skirmishes that once swirled around them are long-forgotten.

Fujairah prides itself on its distinctive characteristics – the way in which modern economic development is taking place without destroying the culture and heritage of the past, and the way in which the pace of its growth is sufficiently well-planned to ensure that the necessary time is taken to assess the impact of new projects before, and not after, they are built.

While its people may, on occasion, look enviously across the mountains to the oil-wealthy emirates in the rest of the country, they are at the same time aware that the ready availability of massive oil revenues has brought with it changes that have all but swept away the past.

In Fujairah, in contrast, no citizen of the emirate need feel that change and development has come so fast that the traditional way of life has disappeared before his or her eyes.

Content, by and large, to progress at a more sedate pace, Fujairah's people have retained the friendliness and hospitality traditional to Arabia, in a way that the visitor, whether from abroad or merely a resident of a

Windsurfers enjoying a dawn sail.

different part of the country, over on a quiet weekend, will come to value.

The holidaymaker who wishes to investigate the possibilities of a little business as well will find no difficulty in doing so. Bodies such as the Chamber of Commerce, the Fujairah Trade Centre and the Fujairah Free Zone Authority are always happy to receive unscheduled visitors with ideas for helping the local economy to continue its growth.

For most, however, Fujairah is a place in which to relax, in which to take stock after a hard week or year of work, in which the quality of life, quite simply, is less frenetic. At the same time, modern facilities are on hand for those who wish to avail themselves of them.

Selected bibliography

Abdullah, MM: *The United Arab Emirates, A Modern History*, 1978
Al Abed, I & Hellyer, P (eds): *The UAE – a New Perspective*, 2001
Anthony, JD: *Arab States of the Lower Gulf*, 1975
Antiquities and Tourism, Department of (Al Ain): *Archaeology in the United Arab Emirates*, Vol 5, 1989
Aspinall, SJ: *Status and Conservation of the Breeding Birds of the UAE*, 1996
Aspinall, SJ (comp): *A Checklist of Birds of Fujairah and the East Coast*, 2002
Bosch, D & Bosch, E: *Seashells of Southern Arabia*, 1989
Chapman, A & Robinson, D: *Birds of Southern Arabia*, 1992
Dipper, F & Woodward, T: *The Living Seas*, 1989
Emirates National History Group, Bulletins No: 1–42, 1977–1990
Gallagher, M & Woodcock, MW: *The Birds of Oman*, 1980
Heard-Bey, F: *From Trucial States to United Arab Emirates*, 1982 and 2005
Hellyer, P (ed): *Waves of Time – The Maritime Heritage of the United Arab Emirates*, 1998
Hellyer, P: *Hidden Riches*, 1998
Information and Culture, Ministry of: Yearbooks and other publications, 1972–2004
Lorimer, JC: *Gazetteer of the Persian Gulf, Oman and Central Arabia*, 1908–1915
Potts, DT, Naboodah, H & Hellyer, P: *Archaeology of the United Arab Emirates: Proceedings of the First International Conference on the Archaeology of the UAE*, 2003
Richardson, C: *The Birds of the United Arab Emirates*, 1989
Swiss-Liechtenstein Foundation for Archaeological Research Abroad: *Archaeological Survey of Fujairah*, 1987
Thomas, RH (ed): *Arabian Gulf Intelligence*, 1985
Journal of the Emirates Natural History Group: *Tribulus*, Vols 1–14, 1991–2004
Western, AR: *The Flora of the United Arab Emirates – An Introduction*, 1989
Zahlan, RS: *The Origins of the United Arab Emirates*, 1978

Acknowledgements

I should like to thank Sheikh Saleh bin Mohammed Al Sharqi, Chairman of the Fujairah Department of Economy and Industry, and others in Fujairah, in particular Abdul Ghafour Behroozian, George Bajk, Abdullah bin Suhail Al Sharqi and Dr Michele Ziolkowski, for their advice, help and suggestions.

Above all, I acknowledge with gratitude the continuing support of Fujairah's Ruler, His Highness Sheikh Hamad bin Mohammed Al Sharqi, who not only stimulated me first to write this book and then to produce the second and third editions, but has also been an invariably courteous mine of information and source of encouragement.

Photographic credits

Al Morda'a, Wafa: 51, 54
Emirates: 20B, 36/37, 91
Fujairah Port: 71, 72/73T
Green, Roy: 19, 30, 57
Haha, Ben: 92
Hellyer, Peter: 21, 27, 46/47, 47, 50B, 52, 53, 67BR, 68/69, 70, 72, 76, 89T, 89B
Hilton Fujairah: 88T, 88B
Kay, Shirley: 62, 77B
Koozan, Younis A: 1, 3, 32T, 41, 50T, 55, 75, 78, 82, 83
Le Meridien Beach Resort: 85, 87
Motivate Publishing: 8, 14, 16, 17

Qureshi, Javed: 74
Sandy Beach Motel: 86
Smith, Steve: 12
Steele, David: Front cover, 4, 5, 7, 8/9, 10/11, 12/13, 18/19, 20T, 22, 24/25, 26, 28, 29T, 29B, 31, 32B, 33, 34/35, 38, 39, 40/41, 42, 44/45, 48, 60, 61T, 61B, 62, 63T, 63B, 64T, 65, 66, 67T, 67BL, 79, 80/81, 90
Western, RA: 6/7, 69
Ziolkowski, Michele and Al Sharqi, Abdullah bin Suhail: Back cover, 23, 43, 45, 49T, 49B, 56/57, 58/59, 64B, 77T, 93

The Author

Peter Hellyer first came to the United Arab Emirates as a documentary film-maker in 1975, staying on to fill a number of government-related posts, most recently as an Adviser in the External Information Department of the Ministry of Information and Culture and as Executive Director of the Abu Dhabi Islands Archaeological Survey (ADIAS).

A former Chairman of the Emirates Natural History Group and a member of the Emirates Bird Records Committee, he has devoted many years of study to the UAE's environment, wildlife, heritage and history, and has published widely on all of these topics.

Though resident with his family in the desert emirate of Abu Dhabi, "which is home," Peter Hellyer has a particular interest in the East Coast and Fujairah where, he notes, "the human and physical environment have retained traditional features that are sadly under threat in much of the rest of the United Arab Emirates."

Author of several books and numerous articles and book chapters on the country's heritage, history and wildlife, he also co-authored *Abu Dhabi – Garden City of the Gulf* and *Al Ain – Oasis City*, two other titles in Motivate's Arabian Heritage series.

THE ARABIAN HERITAGE SERIES

*If you've enjoyed this book you might like to read
some of the other Motivate titles.*

COUNTRY GUIDES

**Bahrain
Island Heritage**
By Shirley Kay

Enchanting Oman
By Shirley Kay

**Kuwait
A New Beginning**
By Gail Seery

Land of the Emirates
By Shirley Kay

**Saudi Arabia
Profile of a Kingdom**
*By various authors
and photographers*

UAE GUIDES

**Abu Dhabi –
Garden City of the Gulf**
*By Peter Hellyer and
Ian Fairservice*

**Al Ain –
Oasis City**
*By Peter Hellyer and
Rosalind Buckton*

**Fujairah –
An Arabian Jewel**
By Peter Hellyer

**Portrait of
Ras Al Khaimah**
By Shirley Kay

**Sharjah –
Heritage and Progress**
By Shirley Kay

NATURAL HISTORY

Birds of the Southern Gulf
*By Dave Robinson
and Adrian Chapman*

**Falconry and Birds
of Prey in the Gulf**
*By David Remple and
Christian Goss*

Sketchbook Arabia
By Margaret Henderson

The Living Seas
*By Frances Dipper
and Tony Woodward*

**The Oasis: Al Ain Memoirs
of 'Doctora Latifa'**
By Gertrude Dyck

ARABIAN HERITAGE GUIDES

**Beachcombers' Guide
to the Gulf**
By Tony Woodward

**Off-Road
in Oman**
*By Heiner Klein
and Rebecca Brickson*

**Off-Road
in the Emirates**
By Dariush Zandi

**Off-Road
in the Emirates 2**
By Dariush Zandi

**Off-Road
in the Hejaz**
*By Patrick Pierard
and Patrick Legos*

On Course in the Gulf
By Adrian Flaherty

**The Green Guide
to the Emirates**
By Marycke Jongbloed

The Off-Roader's Manual
By Jehanbaz Ali Khan

Further titles are available. For more information visit our website:

booksarabia.com